Mid-life

Notes from the Halfway Mark

Elizabeth Kaye

D1509056

Addison-Wesley Publishing Company

Reading, Massachusetts   Menlo Park, California

New York   Don Mills, Ontario   Wokingham, England

Amsterdam   Bonn   Sydney   Singapore   Tokyo   Madrid

San Juan   Paris   Seoul   Milan   Mexico City   Taipei

Library of Congress Cataloging-in-Publication Data

Kaye, Elizabeth, 1945–
Mid-life : notes from the halfway mark / Elizabeth Kaye.
p. cm.
ISBN 0-201-40849-X
1. Middle aged women—United States. 2. Kaye, Elizabeth, 1945– .
I. Title.
HQ1059.5. U5K39 1995
305.4—dc20 94-40336
CIP

Copyright © 1995 by Elizabeth Kaye

Portions of this book have appeared, in somewhat different form, in the *New York Times, Esquire, California* magazine, and *Seven Days.*

Jacket design by Jean Seal
Jacket photograph by Barry David Marcus
Text design by Janis Owens
Set in 11-point Berling by DIX!

1   2   3   4   5   6   7   8   9-DOH-98979695
First printing, February 1995

For Clive

1

~ My sister and I used to joke about growing old. We lived together then, the two of us and one cat, and we would picture ourselves many years and several cats later, fossilized into the barely ambulatory creatures we had assisted across city streets in that distant past.

Age, as we imagined it, would leave us unmellowed, unchastened, our more irksome qualities clear and intact, psychic equivalents of flies trapped in amber.

Moreover, our shoulders would appear to be growing together, our teeth would spend the night in liquid solutions, and we would proceed laboriously from one room to another to accomplish tasks we would fail to remember once we got there.

For a time, these scenarios supplied a certain perverse entertainment.

I knew I had entered mid-life when they no longer seemed amusing.

~ When I became obsessed with middle age, aging was not supposed to be a problem.

In the final decades of the twentieth century, rational women were not expected to agonize about growing older. They were expected to exult in getting better.

"You're fifty now and just hitting your stride," ran the triumphant wording of a vitamin ad. In premillennium mid-life, it was appropriate to take vitamins and get on with it; it was not appropriate to succumb to an unseemly mid-life crisis.

Yet that is precisely what happened to me, and the time I want to tell you about began shortly after my thirty-fifth birthday. I fell subject to a sorrow then, the cause of which was not immediately apparent.

This sorrow would visit in the morning when I walked through Rustic Canyon on the periphery of Santa Monica, shielded by the dense, deep shade cast by groves of eucalyptus. It would visit in late afternoon when I drove homeward through slanting sunlight, toward the stately coconut palms that edge the Palisades and the Pacific Ocean beyond them, phosphorescent in the distance.

At those moments, I would recall four words from a Robert Frost poem: "Nothing gold can stay."

Those words came to me repeatedly, unbidden.

I had learned them years before. When I was thirty-five, I began to learn what they mean.

People spoke of growing old. *Grow* was the wrong word. You didn't grow; you didn't evolve. You were catapulted from one state of being to the next. In one moment, you were a child sprinting along the hot white sand to splash about in chill seawater; in the next, you wore a taffeta dress and gardenia corsage and were setting off for your high school prom; and then there was the moment after that, when you opened your kitchen door to a teenage delivery boy who called you ma'am. And it all seemed to advance as swiftly as a time-lapse sequence of a single rose opening, blooming, and dying.

I had experienced sorrowing times before, but this was more extreme than at those other times. What you feel can be less important than when you feel it. A rain that coaxes forth lilacs in May has an entirely different aspect from a rain that soaks dry leaves at the close of November.

2

~ I still recall the first time someone my age lamented that she no longer looked as she once did. We were both in our early thirties, and I had no idea what she was talking about. In those days, in the Wonderland where I played Alice, aging was a commonplace that only beset others.

"You think you'll never grow old," a friend told me twenty-five years ago. And she was right. I didn't. At the time, this friend was the age I am currently, and the first person I knew to have what is called "a little work."

The work was a face-peel. Afterward, I paid her a visit and tried to ignore that I was attempting to hold up my end of a debate over whether fresh strawberry pie was better at Marie Callender's or at Du Par's with a person who appeared to have been dipped in a vat of crab boil. How could you subject yourself to that? I wondered. As I say, I was young.

And though I was adept at denying I was growing older, even to myself, I was discovering that an efficient way to induce the willies is to subtract your age from your life expectancy.

Gradually, I became familiar with the particulars of aging. I became an avid student of them. I grew absorbed with pamphlets that detailed the antiaging properties of beta-carotene. I studied the benefits and pitfalls of Retin-A and glycolic acid peels and collagen injections. I watched the television program on which Geraldo Rivera, child of the sixties, had his own fat injected into the frown line between his eyebrows.

I became a font of useful information. I knew that young faces are full because they retain water, which later evaporates like puddles of rain in the midday sun. And I knew that 1-800-300-VEIN, a number that seared itself into my memory, was the number to call for help in eradicating veins that had become unsightly.

I did not have unsightly veins but was expecting them any day, just as I expected to fall asleep and awaken utterly changed—cheeks fallen toward my nose, eyes blanketed with fleshy folds, an alien creature on whom age had descended as suddenly and thoroughly as fog enshrouding a harbor.

∼ I began to notice women who seemed to have difficulty with growing older. They were hard to miss. Their hair would be too permed or their lipstick too purple, or they would walk along Venice Beach in Day-Glo bikinis, the Metro section of the *Los Angeles Times* strategically placed over their stomachs' soft flesh.

I heard about a former beauty queen who wept for days after discovering a new wrinkle on her neck. I did not welcome new wrinkles either, though I had begun to believe that those of us who fret about crow's-feet and cellulite and thinning hair were like passengers aboard the *Titanic*, knowing the ship was going down, unable to contend with the dark, unfathomable waiting sea, and cursing instead that one tenth of the iceberg they could see sticking out of the water.

Once I entered mid-life, the *Titanic* as metaphor became a construct that often came to mind, and I would think about the numbing terror that must have enveloped the ship as the final lifeboat departed and the remaining passengers stood on deck, stilled by the dreadful knowledge that there would be no more survivors. This was the foreboding that comes with knowing that all that is born must die.

In much the same way, it struck me when I entered mid-life, we fixate on the specifics of aging because they are easier to face than death.

3

~ "I'm forty-three and proud of it," Ivana Trump told a television audience one spring morning. Mrs. Trump brimmed with the requisite feisty spirit, though her unbridled pride in something apparently achieved by breathing in and then out might strike a casual observer as misplaced. These days, many forty-three-year-old women were inclined to jog five miles a day and looked better than they ever had. Still, Mrs. Trump understood what can befall a woman by age forty-three. For those years had made her a certified survivor, courtesy of marriage to a man who proved otherwise engaged.

How many nights must have come and gone as she paced her marble floors in the small hours, a costly negligee barely obscuring the brand-new silicone breasts "the Donald" had paid for but told a reporter he would never touch. In those evenings, Mrs. Trump must have confronted a fundamental truth of mid-life, which is that promises often go unkept.

Once you digested that, you could easily see how the path from youth to middle age veers away from a child's assumption that you will be exempted from the rules and toward the adult's acceptance that rules are applied impartially. And the rules unequivocally state that if you are forty-three, you have probably lived longer than you are going to live.

At that stage, you were not supposed to mourn what you would never accomplish, like speaking Russian or arguing a murder case before a jury or dancing Balanchine's *Agon* with the New York City Ballet. You were not supposed to mind that you were old enough to be the parent of Holden Caulfield. Nor were you to notice, if you flirted with waiters or garage attendants to get better service, that you had exceeded the age at which flirting availed.

Mid-life required a flair for making necessity a virtue. It called for convincing yourself that life does indeed begin at forty and for seeking inspiration from those who achieved a productive old age, the one fellowship that made brethren of Eudora Welty, Giuseppe Verdi, and the Ayatollah Khomeini.

I wished I could assume the attitude of some people I knew, who navigated mid-life's nascent stages by ingesting massive doses of vitamin E and pretending that turning forty wasn't really all that different from turning thirty. This was an inevitable self-deception among adults who once believed that no one over thirty could be trusted, a conviction that had conferred stature on any twenty-two-year-old with a string of love beads or ready access to some dynamite Tijuana Gold.

I had believed it, too. But it was amazing how the simple act of aging could persuade you that youth worship had been a canard all along. Still, it had been a potent canard, and it had left an entire generation of women and men less prepared to confront middle age than any generation since the Jazz Age.

Wittingly or not, this generation had lived by F. Scott Fitzgerald's dictum that "there are no second acts in American lives," including among their icons the doomed, ever-youthful Janis Joplin, Jim Morrison, and James Dean, and among their catch-phrases "The good die young," "Burn don't rust," and, ultimately, "If I had known I was going to live this long, I'd have taken better care of myself." It was, in other words, a generation apt to discount that Fitzgerald himself sought to raise the second-act curtain just before his death at the age of forty-four, toiling urgently on *The Last Tycoon*, at a desk with a paperweight that bore the legend Business Is Good.

When my mother reached mid-life, she took to marking time in terms of other people's disasters —before Bob was diagnosed with cancer, when Jill was in the hospital, after Eleanore died. I was never sure if these losses loomed more horribly for themselves or for what they betokened of a nonnegotiable future. I had yet to sustain similar disasters, but I never doubted that there was a lot to grieve for.

4

∿ In the long-gone days when I breakfasted on amphetamines and tie-dyed my sheets so they would look like the ocean, there was—in keeping with the general tone of these other activities—a line in *Walden* I particularly liked. "As if you could kill time," Thoreau had written, "without injuring eternity." But though I liked this line, it did not save me from anything. And even then, my extensive injuring of eternity had been spurred by the delightfully self-serving notion that it made no difference what I did, since there would be plenty of time to undo it. It didn't matter how many Saturday nights I squandered in Topanga Canyon or the Hollywood Hills at parties hosted by women who had just filed for divorce or hennaed their hair, events at which fame-starved journalists detailed the plot line of a screenplay they were writing on spec at the urging of a D-girl who claimed to have influence with a vice-president at MGM while agitated, pale-skinned men in black T-shirts and pegged jeans drank too much Jack Daniels and talked about Marxist revolution while waiting for an out-of-work bass player from Van Nuys to show up with the cocaine.

Nor need I regret hours lost recovering from love affairs I should never have entered into or the two afternoons devoted to shopping for a black mohair sweater I had to have but never wore or the three days spent making calls for a ballerina and her husband who wondered if I could find someone to take over their time-share in a St. Bart's condo they ultimately decided to keep.

"All you've lost," somebody told me, "is time."

I didn't bother to explain that this was precisely what troubled me.

I would try to picture Edith Wharton worrying over matters that preoccupied me. But Mrs.

Wharton concerned herself with architecture and gardening and her correspondence with Henry James, while I agonized over what someone I did not even like had said to me five nights before at the Hamburger Hamlet.

"Seek balance in all things," I repeated like a mantra, "and you will have time to do it all." But balance was not among my talents, and it was clear, in any case, that life does not afford the time to do it all.

Here was what I had time to do, according to a calculation I made the week I turned forty: if I read one book a week, wrote twelve magazine articles a year, saw four movies a month, and ate three meals a day, there would still be time for 1,664 more books, 384 more articles, 1,536 more movies, and 35,040 more meals, provided, that is, that I lived an average lifetime of seventy-two years and was one of the lucky ones who didn't get stung by killer bees or end up in a ten-seater plane that crashed into a mountain wall above the Mojave or get run over by a bicycle rider delivering rush orders of Szechuan noodles.

Still, wasted time was not really an issue, because I was banking on a brighter future, and when it dawned, I would be a noble enactor of self-sustaining clichés: I would see the light, clean up my act, get my show on the road. In this chimerical future, all lapses would be reconstituted into grand successes, each failure alchemized into some humbling and useful Lesson Learned that would stand me in better stead.

And I would forgive all the wasted time by subscribing to the saving view that nothing is ever wasted.

∿ Helpful aphorisms notwithstanding, I sank into an obsession with time, and it became a diagnostic feature of my descent into mid-life crisis. This was not unusual. People in mid-life often become obsessed with time simply because it is passing and because their relation to time is the relation, over the years, that changes most radically. The year that, to a five-year-old, is one fifth of a life assumes a different weight when you are forty.

Days go slowly, but years go fast, and a few passing years could set you down in the Kansas of another lifetime. The quantity of vanished time in my own existence had a surreal aspect, its most disturbing measure being that so little around me corresponded to anything I was raised to expect.

But no matter when you are raised, you are schooled to live in a world that, by the time you are ready to live in it, no longer exists. My grandparents were no more prepared for my parents' divorce than my parents were to have three childless daughters, or than I was to inhabit a world where the average marriage lasts seven years and a member of every other household is enrolled in a twelve-step program.

Now, I could walk past the Park Avenue church in which funeral services were held for Jacqueline Kennedy Onassis and see, near the rectory door, a man asleep beneath a cardboard box imprinted with the words "self-storage." I could go to a Smart Bar and order a brain-enhancing cocktail fortified with twelve amino acids or buy a Totally Hair Barbie doll whose ten and a half inches of hair were made from the synthetic kanekalon or learn from an article in *Cosmopolitan*, which promised "you don't have to look as old as you are," that three ways to attain this desirable condition are liposuction, immunotherapy, and alpha hydroxy lotions.

And I found myself feeling simpatico with a computer programmed to answer the question, "Do you think romantic relations are doomed from the start?" by displaying the following answer: "I do tend to walk around with my head in the clouds."

This was future shock at its most extreme and bizarre. And I failed to see how the life I currently lived could be the same life that began with a fervent wish to be like Doreen on *The Mickey Mouse Club*. But then, the extraordinarily wholesome Doreen could not have forecast her life either, could not have known that her stint as a Mouseketeer would eventually lead her to posing nude for a skin magazine named *Gallery*.

The aspect of time that troubled me most was the way it altered the past itself. Ultimately, we were products of our own embellishments, half-truths, and lies, formed as much by the way we remembered events as by the events themselves.

Consider the book editor who recounted to friends a magical night in the 1950s when he glimpsed, in a London restaurant, a stunningly beautiful woman at a nearby table. As it turned out, she was the future star of *Dynasty*, Joan Collins, and when the editor first told this story, he and Miss Collins had never met. When he next told it, Miss Collins was seated at his table. In a subsequent telling, she was his date.

I appreciated this advanced study in the art of self-suggestion, but it troubled me because I was convinced that people are what they remember and that you cannot truly be yourself unless those memories remained as immutable as fingerprints.

Yet memory is figurative. It seems unlikely,

for example, that when I was eleven I slapped my father across the face after he had informed me that he was leaving my mother. Nor does it seem probable that the aspiring writer I was in my teens wrote poetry while perched in the highest branches of a massive oak tree. Still, this faculty called memory insists I did. But these are not memories in any true sense. They are distillations of what it meant to be myself at a given time: the anger at a cherished father who removed himself from my daily existence; the romance I attached to writing early on. These are the facts, and how much does it matter if around those facts you construct a narrative that is essentially apocryphal?

Actually, it matters a lot. The extent to which memories are subject to revision is the extent to which time robs you of intimacy with yourself. And I could imagine few more alienated conditions than the one into which the bloated, doomed Elvis Presley slipped the week before he died, when he visited his trophy room with its walls of gold records, awards, and citations. "Sometimes," he had said, "it's like all this happened to somebody else."

I had no awards or citations, but I had take-out menus from Chinese restaurants that had gone out of business and a Polaroid picture taken of me by a pretty editorial assistant at *California* magazine who was killed three years later in a car crash. And I had a mahogany box full of diaries containing names of people I could no longer recall but was to meet at the Ginger Man on some distant Thursday or to phone promptly at nine A.M. for some long-forgotten reason.

In this box, I had postcards received over the years, including one addressed to my dog from a woman I no longer spoke to who signed the card with a paw mark. And, I had a letter from a man whose face and personality now elude me that begins: "Ohhh, baby, when are you coming home?"

This box contained relics of my past, and served as Exhibit A for the case that illuminates the curious way that certain things seem so crucial at the time, yet ultimately make no difference.

5

~ As I entered mid-life, I became mesmerized by life's choreography, by the balletic precision with which lives intertwine, by the inexorable entrances and exits of friends and circumstances, lovers and family.

Departing my mother's Christmas party in 1986, my grandfather pressed two hard candies into my hand. These candies were ordered specifically for the holidays in an assortment of primary colors and animal shapes. That night, he gave me a green one in the shape of a horse and a red one shaped like a giraffe, and I took them home and placed them on a living-room table.

Nineteen days later, my grandfather was dead. The candies became distinguished as his final gift. I left them where they were, and slowly they shrank, gathering dust, losing shape. Yet I could not throw them away, this unlikely link between possession and loss, between the past and nothing.

You grew attached to things and you grew attached to people and they disappeared or died, and you had to accept it, though some found this more difficult than others. I knew, for example, an aged woman whose husband died in the 1950s when he was forty-two. She never remarried and never removed his photograph from the darkened silver frame that was the only item on her Victorian nightstand. Now she was eighty-four, and the adored man in the picture was half her age. And I wondered if she dreamed of him, if while she slept they floated together, the barely middle-aged man and the very old lady, airy, Chagall-like figures, hands clasped, garments trailing, forever united in time and endless space.

~ Change is illusion, progress is temporary, hope is for people who know no better. These were my cheery convictions as I entered middle-age. In dreams, I was always rearranging furniture, laboring to propel enormous sofas and armchairs and tables into different groupings that left rooms looking no better or worse than they did before I spent hours changing them. And had you asked me, in those days, what life is about, I might have told you that, in most respects, life is an exercise in the rearrangement of furniture.

"Nothing matters," Louis B. Mayer is supposed to have said the moment before he died. And I could calibrate my state of mind by whether his words struck me, at any given time, as infinitely wise or despairing.

∿ One day I went to the doctor for my annual physical. I answered the questions he asked: I had no nosebleeds, no dizziness, no night sweats, but I did have a habit of repeating to myself the words *Nothing gold can stay* and an engulfing sense of panic each time I considered the future.

I wondered what the doctor knew about

growing old. Many of his patients were old, he told me, and many had once been influential. Now, thanks to miraculous advances in medical care, they could outlive the era of their usefulness. The most difficult aspect of aging, the doctor believed, was being left behind, seeing oneself ignored by people who once would have gone to lengths to be ingratiating.

I knew many older people, too. And many were long past seventy and still claiming to live energetic and rewarding lives. Though I couldn't help speculating as to whether their definition of energetic and rewarding had much in common with mine.

So I asked the doctor what were the odds that when I was seventy I would not be saddened to look back and remember the way I am now.

"Very small," he replied.

6

~ On a morning in early summer, shortly after my forty-third birthday, I was awakened by spasms produced by a herniated disk, brought on by what my thirty-year-old chiropractor helpfully identified as "phase-one degeneration." The problem was unexpected. And though I had seen several friends through serious illness and witnessing their suffering had convinced me that I knew what suffering is, it took my own pain to teach me that this understanding can never be held by those who bring bouquets and chocolates to the sickroom and are free to leave at dinnertime.

Every ailing person knows there is a dominion of the sick and of the well and that they have nothing in common. An Italian family in black mourning garb gathers around a corpse at a Bleecker Street funeral parlor while, three doors away, account executives shop at the Banana Republic for white linen outfits to wear on mild weekends in Rhinebeck.

Everywhere, hidden from view, are frail women and men who wait indoors on a sunny day for an emissary from the real world. And when I became one of them, it was as if I were existing in a place I had seen postcards of, but never expected to visit. In the world of the well, people complain because the waiter is slow or because there is nothing they care to see at the Sixplex. In the world of the sick, there is only pain and terror and getting through them.

There are no safe havens for the weak and infirm. But cities, with their special reverence for speed and power, can seem unremittingly cruel to those who are slow and powerless. And during the summer that I became slow, living in Manhattan and accessorized for the season in a brand-new white neck brace and sling, each journey from my apartment became a bizarre and treacherous ordeal. I was intimidated by the ferocity with which people walked and by the milling clumps they formed at corners and by roller skaters who materialized from nowhere and by cars that always seemed driven by angry drivers.

On some days, I would sit on a bench or ride a bus and try to look people in the eye. I wanted what a person often wants when they're confined to bed for most of the day, which is a moment of contact with another human soul. But no one met my gaze. Instead, they averted their eyes. Sometimes this made me angry. At other times it filled me with a terrible sadness. I had become an unwilling trespasser in the land of the nearly invisible old, and it was as if I had entered a covenant with them, with all the men and all the women who no longer are what they were before and are consigned to be ignored by everyone who cannot face the people who have become what they dread most.

Illness is a fine teacher. It simplifies, clarifies, distilling everything. I intended to remember all it taught, but with its absence came a partial amnesia.

Still, I did learn several things that I am not likely to forget. I learned that the human body can be formidable and punishing and resilient. And I learned for a dead certainty that it is not built to last.

~ In the winters, when I was small, my grandparents took me to Palm Beach. We stopped going there when I was eleven. Thirty-five years later, while I was convalescing from what proved to be three years of back pain, I returned for a brief visit by myself. I am not sure what I was looking for, but what I found was that Palm Beach is a bad place to search for epiphanies but a good place to get a rest. I wanted to rest. By then, I had a marriage that was ending and too many people I loved were dead. Rest implied a beginning when so much signified an end.

Each morning, I rode a bike along Lake Worth path, past the Whitehall, the fifty-two-room mansion patterned on the Vatican and Versailles and described upon its completion in 1902 as North

America's Taj Mahal. The Whitehall is currently a museum, but it was converted to a hotel in the 1920s, and it was there that I stayed with my grandparents.

Originally, the Whitehall was built to be the winter home of Henry Flagler, a founder of Standard Oil, who developed the Florida coast in the 1880s, coaxing a retreat for the rich from an alligator wallow where Seminole Indians had once speared abalone and copperheads curled beneath the frangipani and early settlers fashioned shelters from splintery wood salvaged from shipwrecks.

The mansion Flagler devised for himself featured a vast entry hall with a baroque ceiling embellished by hand-painted panels symbolizing Prosperity and Happiness, and dominated by the imposing Italian-marble staircase on which Flagler took the fall that precipitated his death.

Imagine it: The old man, aged into delicacy, edges up the expansive staircase toward his Louis XV bedroom, where furniture and walls are draped in yellow watered-silk damask. His bony feet, shielded by green velvet slippers, falter on the gleaming marble. He tumbles downward and is broken by his own staircase, whose very height was intended to emblematize his immunity to everyday disasters. There he lay, undiscovered for several hours, in the house that he ordered be built so huge that his absence could go unnoticed by all of its other inhabitants.

When I heard this story, I was in my early forties, and it was entirely in tune with life as I had come to perceive it, though its special ironies would have had no place in the sweet and orderly world of the child my grandparents took to Florida.

7

~ In my youth I believed that anything was possible. I did not believe in cause and effect. I was certain that at any moment, I might be offered a seven-year contract at Warner Brothers or a two-month cruise to Tahiti or first prize in a contest I had neglected to enter. I was convinced that the prospect of sudden change waited around each corner. I went to the Empire State Building prepared to turn and see the man of my dreams taking in the sharp-edged skyline with the passionate, steady gaze of Gary Cooper playing Howard Roark. When I reached mid-life, I still believed in sudden change, but not the sort that enabled me to envision a chance encounter with my dream man on a rooftop.

The sort of sudden change in which I had come to believe was of a type I witnessed one spring afternoon when a delivery truck spun out of control on Park Avenue, skidding noisily, hurtling into the air, then flipping over and landing upside down with a tremendous thud in the center divider, atop a bed of carefully tended bright-red tulips.

The driver was miraculously alive, but in the moments immediately following the crash, none of the passersby knew this. The dog walker clutching the leashes of five eager puppies, the young woman cradling an armload of forsythia branches, the father and son in their Yankee caps—all stopped, waited, and stared. A supporting cast, they were augmented by the usual principals: the photographer who materializes from nowhere, the policemen, the EMS team, all circling the truck in a matter of moments, as if the city were poised for disaster, ready to feed on it, incorporate it, revel in it.

And at their center, the hapless driver, proving that the slender bar between the secure world and the world where no one is safe can be breached in a single moment. Strapped to a stretcher, eyes shut, covered by a dark-gray blanket reddened with blood from his shoulder, he had been plucked from the everyday world where weather reports air promptly at eight minutes past the hour and Associated has tuna on sale for forty-nine cents a can.

~ "People are into channeling," a woman tells me one morning. She is a therapist but seems even more depressed than I am, and we meet in Riverside Park each day at seven A.M. and walk our dogs, two disconsolate women just into middle age, watching their lively pets disport themselves amid the venerable hawthorn trees and providing one of many occasions when I experience my life as a Feiffer cartoon.

People are into channeling, it seems, because they have the same impression I have, which is that living is—to put it simply—much too complicated. And so they turn to channeling and *The*

Course on Miracles and seminars given by Deepak Chopra and yeast-free diets and whatever else they can contrive to allay the aching sense of being rudderless. This sense was extraordinarily widespread, and an astonishing amount of mid-life activity could be understood as an attempt to deny it.

Denying it was the apparent aim of a fortyish woman I sat beside during an E. L. Doctorow reading at Manhattan's Ninety-second Street Y. I had spent enough time alone by then to imagine how she had come to attend this event by herself: the fortuitous spotting of the announcement in the paper, the anxious calls to see if friends were available, the purposeful decision to go alone, the subsequent sending for the ticket—evidence of determination to better oneself along lines prescribed by self-help courses that recommend becoming your own best friend, setting the table when eating alone at home, developing a hobby, and pursuing a wide range of interests.

Her appearance at the Y was thus a small yet significant achievement, but then, minutes into the reading, she dozed off. What will she tell herself

when she awakens? I wondered. Will she be con-
fused, not sure if the radio is on, then remember
that this is the Doctorow reading that loomed as
the main event on her calendar since she bravely
sent for the ticket?

Now, an evening that might have provided an
occasion for self-congratulation had increased the
burden of that dull, enduring sadness called despair. I knew despair. I knew it well. I felt as despairing as it was possible to feel and still pay the
rent, get to superior court by 8:30 A.M. to report a
story, and remember to pick up the dry cleaning.

For years, I had filled notebooks with cheering
aphorisms meant to instill courage and inspire forward motion. "You can't reach the ocean," one
read, "if you're afraid to lose sight of the shore."
But when I entered mid-life, I could no longer bear
to read cheering phrases, just as I could not bear to
read entries I had made over the years in dozens of
journals pledging to try harder and do better.

I did not like being at the mercy of my own
anxiety. And one of the more galling aspects of
this condition was that men seemed so much less

subject to it. Men rarely wasted time as women did, not because they were less anxious, but because their anxiety tended to take more productive forms. I had a male colleague, for example, at *California* magazine whose office was separated from mine by a Sheetrock wall. For a while, we spent evenings together, but eventually these evenings became arduous. The next morning, I would sit in my office, head in hands, deadened as a hunk of limestone, and hear, through that thin wall, the sound of his tapering fingers asserting themselves on his computer keyboard with the staccato insistence of a manic woodpecker.

Similarly, when my marriage began going terminally flat, my husband would appear in the kitchen each morning, fill a thermos with coffee, and return upstairs to his study, where he would spend the next four hours writing.

I was too unnerved by the state of our marriage to sit down, far less write, so I spent those hours in the kitchen, standing at the counter, perfecting my piecrust. By the time the marriage ended, he had written a novel that was nominated for a Pulitzer Prize, while I had become conversant with the precise degree of flakiness that can be obtained with lard or Crisco or margarine.

But then, he had always used his anxiety to read and to learn, while my own anxiety had driven me out on endless walks whose duration was such that the bottoms of my feet bled and needed bandaging. By the time my husband was thirty, he had read many books and discovered many useful and interesting things.

By the time I was thirty, I had discovered something with another sort of usefulness. I had discovered that it is possible to walk with bloody feet.

8

~ Once I entered mid-life, I had a recurring fantasy. I imagined calling my father or mother and asking them what life is about. In these fantasies, both parents had extraordinarily brilliant, ready answers. I could not imagine those answers, but I could imagine the overwhelming relief I felt upon hearing them. Some days I could hardly refrain from making this call. But I never made it, because I did not want to find out that my parents did not have the answer either.

One summer afternoon, I took a walk across the Sheep Meadow in Central Park, where people I knew long ago used to gather for love-ins and other communal al fresco activities like dropping acid and ingesting mushrooms. In the near distance, a man was playing an acoustic guitar and singing "Here, There, and Everywhere" from the Beatles album *Revolver*. His song attracted a woman who had come to the park to watch her teenage sons in a baseball game; it caught the attention of a gray-haired man who secured his Patagonia bag beneath the shaded bench where he sat reading *The Wall Street Journal*. It caught my ear, too, reminding me of summer days when I wore a floppy purple hat, halter top, and bell-bottom jeans and drank Lancers' rosé at cafés where red candles burned in straw-bound Chianti bottles while we talked about why it is preferable to chew hashish rather than smoke it and about how hot to make the iron when ironing your hair and whether we ought to march with the Ho Chi Minh contingent at the antiwar demonstration in Washington.

I could recall hearing "Here, There, and Everywhere" in the sixties, late on another summer day while I prepared a rice dish with dried apricots and cumin for the man I lived with. A slight breeze from the Hudson River passed through our kitchen window, and the song came on the radio, and it was one of those moments *both of us thinking that love never dies* when the paranoia and hysteria that were the sixties could be set aside, and you could feel young and unfettered, and happiness could seem nearer than at any other time.

As a rule, I am not given to crying, but I wept on the afternoon that I heard the man singing "Here, There, and Everywhere" in Central Park. I did not want to, but I could not help it, and once I started weeping, I could not stop. After that, I wept on street corners and in train stations and in movie theaters where they played soft-rock songs before the feature. I wept at songs of loss: at "You Don't Send Me Flowers" and "The Way We Were" and "That's What Friends Are For."

I often thought of the way John Lennon, iconized memory of my youth, finally developed a modest ambition: He wanted to live and make music without going insane. He was forty when he figured out how these goals might be accomplished and was murdered weeks after receiving that revelation. The John Lennon syndrome had a familiar and guiding principle, and it was that just as your goal seems within reach, you are destroyed. This was the Abraham Lincoln syndrome and the Robert Kennedy syndrome, too. And it might induce you to say that life is a grand and glorious existential game or to say that life is futile.

◇ When I thought of learning things too late, I remembered a dinner at the American Film Institute at which a Lifetime Achievement Award was presented to Fred Astaire. One of his leading ladies, Eleanor Powell, recalled rehearsing with Mr. Astaire in the 1930s, when the publicly urbane Astaire was privately at his most savagely driven and perfectionistic.

"Let's do it one more time," he would say. He said it over and over again, and the more he said it, the more Miss Powell wanted to scream. But five decades had come and gone, and Eleanor Powell was sixty-eight years old.

"Oh, Mr. Astaire," she said, "what I wouldn't give to do it one more time."

It was the standard equation: By the time you

understand why youth is wasted on the young,
your youth is gone.

∽ Had you asked what I wanted in the months
when I was crying, I would have told you I wanted
to feel safe. There was only one place I felt safe.
That was in the hushed arrangements of stores. I
loved being in stores, and because I worked at
home, I could begin work by six in the morning,
put in a long day, and still leave the house in time
to hang out in stores for a couple of hours. I could
take pleasure in any type of store: elaborate, over-
priced boutiques where purchases were wrapped
in layers of pink tissue paper and carried home in
shiny tote bags with plump braided cords; stores
that sold flowing scarves fashioned from glowing
chenille and panne velvet; stores that sold soaps
infused with jasmine and coconut oil, or chocolates
shaped like seashells and filled with praline or ha-
zelnut cream.

But the stores I loved most were flower shops
where exquisite bouquets were enclosed in clear

cellophane cones secured with satin ribbons in the pure, bright colors of fresh lavender and Meyer lemons.

I loved the dried roses at Fantasia, the terra-cotta pots planted with lady-slipper orchids at Salou, the ceramic urns filled with magnolia boughs at Surroundings, the crystal vases that brimmed with osianna roses at Renny.

Address cards attached to arrangements were windows into privileged lives. I liked knowing that someone was sending Casablanca lilies to Kimberly Farkas and that Judith Peabody was about to receive two dozen Anna roses interspersed with white French lilacs.

And I loved department stores where you could observe an unending variety of shoppers: teenage girls with short, sculpted hair and black leather jackets, leaning on cosmetics counters while debating the relative merits of spice and nutmeg lip pencils; white-haired widows attempting to occupy an afternoon by rummaging through a sale of Italian leather handbags; elegant Korean ladies in three-piece Valentino suits, retreating into mirrored fitting rooms to try on floor-length satin gowns cut on the bias.

Stores had their own select universe, and tapping into it was not hard. I simply placed my name on mailing lists and received, in return, engraved invitations to private sales of summer silks and shearling coats, to the Donna Karan trunk show, to personalized consultations with fashion experts, to meet the creative force behind Prescriptives.

At perfume and makeup counters, I filled out cards that yielded later contact. "As a valued Bergdorf customer," read a card that arrived in the mail one morning, "there's a wonderful free gift with purchase waiting for you." In the world I longed for, all customers were valued and every gift was free and purchase was not necessary to its procurement.

In stores, life seemed comprehensible. Existence proceeded sensibly, driven by immutable order. Selection was followed by purchase, money was exchanged for goods. I was soothed by these simple and basic transactions, and even more by their subtext: that life can be bettered by the right object. This was a profoundly seductive notion, and I felt intense relief in the presence of salespeople who either subscribed to it or were paid to pretend they did. These people displayed an unequivocalness that can be appreciated only by the deeply equivocal. "Nobody does matte jersey like Harriet Selwyn," they would say, or "This little accessory makes an outfit."

And though I had trouble sustaining faith in the curative powers of little accessories, the possibility that some people did maintain that faith lent me an obscure sense of hope.

"The little $12,500 bag is such a hit," reads an item I carried in my wallet for a year after clipping it from an issue of *Mirabella*, "Bergdorf's can't keep it in stock."

But when I was in stores, there were things I had to forget. I had to forget the way shoppers seek to purchase what money cannot buy or went to stores for the reason I did, which was to ease memory and soothe apprehension about the future.

And I needed to forget how worthy goals can be displaced in a quest for the perfect mandarin silk blouse or any item brought forth more easily than a sonnet or a watercolor of bathers on a river bank.

I knew a gifted writer who was always buying English china, then agonizing over whether to keep it or take it back. She wanted to write an important novel and seemed to have the talent to do it. But you can have the talent for many things and still be so daunted by the exertion they demand that you settle for applying your creative gifts to the pressing question of whether or not to return the Spode dessert plates.

～ One afternoon, I wandered into a pizza parlor where a children's party was taking place complete with a chocolate sheet cake piled with blue and white icing and a harlequin and a clown impersonated by actors who may have dreamed of playing Hamlet or Macbeth but were nonetheless entertaining a gathering of overfed seven-year-olds at Original Ray's Pizza on Columbus Avenue and Eighty-third Street. Wanting to be an actor but becoming a clown seemed, in those days, as reasonable a metaphor for mid-life as any.

I glanced in the harlequin's direction. He lifted a boy and girl onto his lap and placed them on his knees. The children looked enthralled. To them, the world must have seemed an enchanted and sunny place. I wondered why it did not seem that way to me. But I knew the answer. For I had concluded, by then, that the nameless sorrow adults are disposed to feel is produced by the fact that life does not turn out to be what we think it will be when we are young enough to sit in the harlequin's lap.

In my entire circle, there was only one person whose life had proceeded in precisely the way I was taught lives are meant to proceed. He had married the same day of the same year that I had married, but while my marriage faltered, his produced two beautiful children currently being raised by his lovely and unusually self-sufficient wife, who rode horses each afternoon and presided over their tasteful but not at all ostentatious home near the Hudson River in Dobbs Ferry.

He told me about his life. He showed me the children's pictures. Normality seemed so rare that its presence struck me as intriguing and exotic. Of course, I was cynical enough that I half-expected to hear that he had abandoned his wife and run off with an eighteen-year-old belly dancer or had had a sex-change operation prior to absconding with the company funds to Tasmania.

Still, I thought of him often: the two perfect children, the lovely wife, the contented existence. "I'm just back from Disney World," he told me one Monday morning.

"Who isn't?" I said.

9

~ Things happen and they cannot be undone: This is something I prefer not to believe, but even now, with mid-life sorrow far behind me, it remains the one fixed truth my experience suggests. For example, certain things happened to me when I was a child so that, later, trust did not come easily to me and I was apprehensive each time I saw a grown man display affection to a small girl. A grandfather raising a three-year-old into the air; a father securing his baby's diaper, his hands uncertain, his face intent; a five-year-old perched in her uncle's lap: I could assure myself that these scenarios were altogether benign, yet in private renderings they were etched in menace. Call it a phobia or a learned response. It was both, and it had become ingrained. Like many wounds, it could be bandaged or ignored or partly mended, but never fully healed.

All this came into sharp relief shortly after my marriage in the early eighties, while my husband and I summered in western Massachusetts in a rented federal-era house that had sun-faded wallpaper patterned with jonquils and a mahogany sleigh bed covered by a quilt in a Dresden-plate pattern.

Everything in that house comforted me except for an oil painting above the bed depicting an aged, bearded fisherman guiding a small wooden boat through a turbulent sea, his arm sheltering a frightened little girl.

Paintings like this were for sale in souvenir galleries throughout the Cape, in unduly elaborate frames with small bronze plaques declaring the work's title to be *The Kindly Fisherman* or *Rescue*. But in the Rorschach test my mind supplied, the young girl was not being rescued. She was being carried out to sea for purposes that could only be sinister. And so, throughout the early months of my marriage, I tried not to look at that painting above the bed.

Each day, late in the afternoon, my husband and I started up a pebbly path edged by slender birches, where remnants of stone fences gave way to a narrow trail beside a beaver pond. The air was cooled by deep shade, and in the near distance, amid lush black pines and clumps of scrub oaks and groupings of stunted cedars, you could see the stone-and-mortar foundation of the two-story wooden house where my husband's family once gathered for holidays and summers.

In those days, there had been a whitewashed porch where collies took refuge from the heat and a wobbly stand filled with the walking sticks my husband's grandfather carved from knotty branches of hickory and ash. A faded green hammock had been secured to upright maples by thick knots of hemp, and suppers of fresh-picked tomatoes and corn and blackberries were served on white dishes trimmed with hand-painted pale-pink roses. It was a house that had less to do with life as it is than with the life of dreams, life as we wish to imagine it and as it appears on those occasions when the world seems brushed by magic.

This house was intended to be handed down through the generations. But as things turned out, it was sold abruptly in 1956 when the Yankee Atomic Electric Company was authorized to build one of the nation's first nuclear-power plants on a site less than a mile away and began buying up all the property within a one-mile radius. The Yankee company got hold of the house, then leveled it unceremoniously, leaving only the foundation to serve as a dank breeding ground for poplars and the assertive ferns that fanned across what had been the basement.

Sitting on the edge of this foundation, my husband and I talked of turning back the encroaching sumac, harbinger of an Eden lost, of wilderness reclaimed. We pictured the house we could build here, where the old one had been. I looked forward to these speculations and never voiced what had for me become their essential feature: that the plans symbolized what I hoped the marriage would do, which was to superimpose new life over signs of ruin.

You will understand what I believed, at that time, about the likelihood of happy endings when I tell you that I was not astonished that the graft my marriage represented failed to take. And as the years passed, I spent my time in the city and avoided our vacation home in a rural upstate town, with its wood stove, pine rafters, and eyebrow windows from which the dog and cat yearned after woodchucks that invaded the compost heap. On the first day of summer, some six years following our wedding, my husband drove me to the station in Albany so that I could take the four o'clock train to Manhattan. We waited at a Formica table in the snack bar, sipping lemonade and reading local papers, and as the train left the station, he waved at me and I waved at him and it was friendly enough for a marriage that had come to have its share of unfriendly days. Neither of us suspected that I would never again sleep in the white iron bed we had found at the Newfane flea market on a Sunday drive and

taken home after securing it with fishing line to the
roof of the car—back when doing those things together seemed to be the point of everything.

But, in fact, because things happen, I never
saw the upstate house again. I could never return
to places I once belonged but no longer did, places
that had slipped into the haunted netherland we
designate as "before." I tried not to live in before,
and I tried not to live in that future known as
"after." And so, over time, I abandoned valued
belongings rather than face the sorrow that might
accompany their retrieval. In an Amagansett beach
house I left an antique purple silk kimono embroi-
dered with tangerine-colored flowers; in Malibu
Canyon, I left my entire record collection, including
all my 45s; in a Palm Springs motel room I left three
Bakelite bracelets in graduated tones of yellow. This
was the trail behind me, bread crumbs to my particular Gretel, and to follow it was to risk reimmersion
in a past that had already proven unworkable.

Among possessions left in that upstate house
were an asparagus cooker used by my grandmother's cook, two toaster ovens that didn't work, and

a pale-blue enamel pitcher purchased at Nonesuch Antiques in the early eighties, when I lived on the edge of Los Angeles, in Ocean Park.

I bought that pitcher during what I suspect will have been the precise center of my life, the balancing point between young and old, the private equinox in which light and dark are of equal length. As proof of this hypothesis, I was engaged in simultaneous flirtations with my agent's boss and male secretary, the former, a wandering family man in his early fifties, the latter, a twenty-two-year-old who had just graduated from Yale. That summer, through searing heat waves and the requisite smog and damp ocean breezes, I filled the blue pitcher with gladiolus—long, brave stalks heavy with blossoms of pale violet, peach, and yellow—and placed it, in anticipation of male visitors, on a pine washstand near the doorway.

In the fall, I moved to New York and met the man I would marry. A few months later, men from Bekins Moving and Storage packed the pitcher in the sports section of a week-old *Los Angeles Times*, and carted it, along with all my worldly possessions, first to a warehouse in the Bronx and then to the apartment my husband and I rented near Riverside Drive.

That summer, I brought the pitcher to the country house and placed it on a lace-covered table on my husband's side of the bed, and for the next four years I filled it with wisteria and lilac branches and the iridescent-blue delphiniums I had planted so they could be seen from the kitchen windows. Then the country house no longer featured in my routines. I next saw the pitcher three years after my husband and I had separated, by which point a difficult marriage had been recast as the friendship it should always have been and my delphiniums were being watered by another woman.

The man to whom I had been married often photographed the house. Eventually I asked to see some pictures and discovered that my study had been converted into a playroom for his new wife's young daughter. Sketches drawn by the little girl and her mother were tacked to the wall, and several of these were of the pale-blue pitcher, proud still-life model, positioned in the center of the room, brimming with delicate bluebells and Queen Anne's lace.

The progression of all this was logical, but it did not make any sense. And to have things make sense, to elevate them beyond the merely random, these were my preoccupations as I entered the years that are supposed to be one's prime. This entire exercise had about it the certainty of failure, for I had long since begun to fear that nothing made sense, to suspect most things to be random, and to have little patience for people who used words like *prime*.

Yet much as mid-life troubled me, I would not have wished to go back and be the person I was in my twenties, that young woman given to a manner so lost and vague that people terminated conversations with me by saying, "Get some sleep" or by wishing me good luck.

I had been desperate to learn things in those earlier days but spent less time learning than castigating myself for what I did not know, though on occasion I enrolled in evening courses and there studied the Boxer Rebellion and the history of primitive figurines and made a list of 100 things all primates know.

To effect further self-betterment, I resolved to swim a mile each day, to drink yeast in my grapefruit juice, to study the lives of leaders of the French Revolution. I compiled lengthy lists of books to read, people to write, places to visit, money spent. I listed items required for trips to Memphis or Blue Hill, Maine, sites supplying the riverbank or seaside setting where life might proceed smoothly along that extraordinarily interesting course I had in mind.

"Don't forget silver stockings" reads a yellowing note to myself in purple ink. In the world I yearned for, the possibility of total control was always in reach, and an absolute correlation existed between prospects for happiness and whether or not you remember to pack the silver stockings.

Awash in Walter Mitty fantasies, I booked passage twice on the *France* and once on the *United States* but was too apprehensive to venture that far and canceled the bookings. At times, though, I encountered women who lived the adventures I imagined, who had just returned from a cruise up the Nile or a month in a beach shack with no electricity on the Caribbean side of Antigua.

One of these women was an aspiring photographer who had bobbed hair, a tiny apartment on the quai Voltaire, and an intimate friendship with Milos Forman. I worked up the courage to invite her to dinner, and when she accepted, I roasted a chicken and chilled a good white wine, but the hours passed and the wine got warm and the chicken got cold, and I sank into self-recrimination when I realized she wasn't coming.

I knew, by then, that the Boxers' uprising failed when the rebels were decimated by the combined opposition of Russians, Americans, and Europeans. I knew a pre-Columbian icon from an albarello. I knew how to oppose my thumb to the rest of my hand and ninety-nine other things all primates know. But I did not know the first thing about how to live, and so did not know that if someone treats you rudely, the failure is not necessarily yours.

I had managed to change since then. I am not

sure how, I cannot say when, since change is so imperceptible as it occurs that only a backward glance, in Edith Wharton's phrase, can reveal its presence. But after this change took place, the rhythms of my life felt easy and appropriate, though what seemed appropriate to me had little relation to appropriateness in the sense in which I initially understood that word.

Yet, in many regards, I hadn't changed and was still the person in the photograph my mother took when I was four years old of me and my very first boyfriend. My boyfriend was five. He has his arm around me. I have Buster Brown bangs and am clutching an Oreo cookie in my right hand and look so happy that my eyes are practically crossed.

This girl in the picture grew up to be a troublesome creature and a person I have variously sought to disown and leave behind. Yet I have a fondness for that little person, and this is just as well. For she is someone I am consigned to take with me everywhere, because things happen and cannot be undone.

10

~ Like most American children raised in the 1950s, I was schooled in those perky Dale Carnegie verities that assure that the race is to the swift and that the early bird gets the worm. But when I reached mid-life, I had lived long enough to note that early birds can choke on worms they swallow and that the swift can end up with splinted bones. What I was taught mattered less, finally, than what I knew, and one thing I knew was that things happen and the fallout is often not pretty.

I imagined people I saw at luncheonettes and bus stops as they must have looked as children, when they were new and the disappointments that would harden their features had not yet overtaken them.

The more suffering I saw, the more I seemed to see, though I never knew if this was because there were, in fact, more suffering people, or because I was more aware of them.

A young man I met had watched his brother commit suicide by jumping off the Brooklyn Bridge and since then had fantasized about setting houses on fire so that he could extinguish the flames and be a hero. I read a letter written to Ann Landers by a woman with postsurgical scarring who called herself Zero Self-Esteem in Chicago. "When I look in the mirror," she wrote, "I see a forty-eight-year-old woman who will probably never again have intimate contact with a man."

On *The Sally Jesse Raphael Show*, guests were identified by helpful supers that read: "Molested by priests" or "Attacked by snakes." They recounted their victimization to millions of viewers, an orgy of self-revelation affirming that the sideshow was being played in the main tent. One guest was a forty-four-year-old woman with a butch haircut, a cropped Grateful Dead T-shirt, and a compulsion to defend her marriage to a fourteen-year-old.

"I don't see him as fourteen," she explained. "I see him as a wonderful person."

You could not hear many of these stories without noting that by the time people entered mid-life, they could be bruised in myriad ways and destined to be stitched together by sutures that barely held: fifty-year-old housewives numbed by their husbands' indifference, seeking comfort in a dog-eared copy of *The Road Less Traveled* or fantasies about Mel Gibson; former hippies whose hypnotherapy produced the revelation that they had, twenty years earlier, been sexually abused by their swamis.

And then there were the legions of women and men relying on therapists to locate the forgotten trauma that would account for all subsequent lapses, deficiencies, and insecurities. This urge was one I respected, though I was wary of its failure to take into account the tyranny of the everyday, those routine breaches of attention and regard whose effects could be brutal and cumulative.

In the early eighties, I wrote a piece in which I made some weak joke about the difficulty of remaining ambulatory in a crippling world.

"Why crippling?" a man wrote from El-
dersbergh, Maryland. "It really matters to me."

I kept his letter, thinking I would answer it,
transferring it, as years went by, from the back of
one datebook to another, but I never wrote him
because I simply did not know what to say.

Maybe I should have told him about an event
I attended at an American Legion Hall on the East
End of Long Island whose purpose was to raise
money for a sweet-faced forty-nine-year-old local
fisherman whose pretty wife was in the final stages
of cancer and whose eighteen-year-old daughter
had lapsed into an irreversible coma.

The fisherman was well-liked in the community, and everyone turned out and danced to Marvin
Gaye's "Can I Get a Witness" and ate meatballs on
fancy toothpicks and celery stuffed with peanut
butter. Among them were two of the fisherman's
childhood friends. When they'd been young, they
had called themselves the Three Musketeers. They
ran races through potato fields and, later, at the high
school prom, stood balanced on each other's shoulders as a photographer snapped their picture.

One of these men was now the community's Babbitty chief of police. The other man had never quite found his footing. And there was the fisherman himself, who was being robbed of everything that mattered to him. Once, life had seemed bright and promising to them. But that was long ago. The fisherman attempted to smile as he secured a thick arm around each man's shoulder.

"Well, here we are," he said. "The Three Musketeers. Together again."

~ HARRISBURG, Penn., April 6, 1969 (UPI) —"A man went on a shooting spree with a high-powered rifle on the Pennsylvania Turnpike today, killing two persons and wounding fifteen others. He then shot and killed his wife and himself. The man was identified as Donald Lambright, 31 years old, with addresses in Philadelphia, St. Louis, and Cleveland. He was the son of the comedian Stepin Fetchit."

That was the lead to a story on page one of the *New York Times*. For twenty years, I kept it pinned to the wall above my desk, though for many of those years I failed to understand what, aside from the obvious, intrigued me about it. It finally dawned on me that the story of Donald Lambright verified the paradigm I found most basic, which is that you spend the first part of your life being young and the rest of it paying for that experience.

By this reasoning, it was not startling that a son of the professionally obsequious Stepin Fetchit became entrapped in rage and violence, any more than it seemed odd that the brutally neglected Norma Jean would seek to transform herself into Marilyn Monroe, object of popular fantasy. Things happen and they lead to other things. That part of it was not complicated.

What baffled me was how much of all this was inescapable, what portion of your fate was determined by what you did and how much by what was done to you. Either way, crawling out from beneath the primal load was no pastime for the fainthearted, and I felt kinship with anyone who attempted to short-circuit that process by playing a one-armed bandit in Las Vegas or buying five dozen lottery tickets or waiting at the stage door for the band. These were the disappointed people whose secret weariness precluded sustained efforts on their own behalf and so were consigned to the fragile hope that everything can be altered by a single, transforming thought or moment.

"I'm Elizabeth Taylor's son, practically," a homeless man with tuberculosis told a newspaper reporter. This was the sort of wishful delusion I understood, just as I understood the woman who was convinced her life would have been entirely different if Elvis hadn't thought she had been lost in a snowstorm.

To hold these notions was to regard oneself as subject to fate. Others rejected the significance of fate and proceeded according to plan. I, too, made plans, but I had come to perceive experience as an amalgam of intent and happenstance, like pebbles tossed into a pond, followed by successive ripples in the water.

"It's so strange," I found myself saying aloud during those first tentative stages of my reluctant entry into middle age. "It's just so strange," I kept repeating, speaking to no one, apropos of everything.

～ Here is another newspaper item, this one from the front page of the Metro section of the *Los Angeles Times*, Tuesday, February 26, 1980: "Fires Follow Floods—Remains of two homes on Solar Drive in Nicholas Canyon that were destroyed by flames Monday" reads the caption beneath a photograph of an ultramodern hillside home in the Richard Neutra style that had been reduced to a charred ruin, its scorched foundation eerily reflected in an adjacent swimming pool.

"Burned body of a man, believed to be the owner, Cyrus Merton, was found in house above. Damage to both houses was about $700,000; cause was not known."

But I presumed to know the cause of that fire because I had known Cyrus Merton, who was among the first men I knew to descend into mid-life crisis. And so I can trace this fire's origins to the 1970s, when Cyrus Merton reached mid-life and it became apparent that he was ill equipped for this inevitability. Soon, he was employing hair spray to reinforce the thinning locks carefully arranged across his bald spot, another white-haired businessman with rose-tinted aviator glasses and half a dozen pairs of Nike running shoes and an overwhelming fear of being excluded from enlivening cultural innovations like drug abuse and wife-swapping.

If this condition was familiar, so were his solutions to them. Shedding his first family, he began a second one with a wife the approximate age of his children. He took to starting each day with a three-mile jog through the canyon, followed by a tumbler of fresh-pressed carrot juice sipped while deepening his tan in the Jacuzzi. Along the way were the obligatory passes at his wife's friends; the midnight dinners at Dan Tana's, where someone was usually face down in the pasta; the poolside evenings at home during which he sought to persuade the guests who smoked his dope and downed his tequila into a nude, midnight swim.

His young wife, no more immune to the era's so-
cial rituals, eventually left him to "find herself," a
sojourn involving yoga and a succession of younger
men and other anticonventional habits she maintained with Cyrus Merton's alimony payments.

Increasingly, her former husband's anxiety to
remain hip took the form of too much drinking
and pot smoking. And when these activities ceased
to redeem and began generating their own misery,
he attempted to shake them, but by then his addic-
tion was entrenched. The night he burned to
death, it seems, he had been drinking in bed and
had fallen asleep with a lit cigarette between his
fingers.

A washout on Nicholas Canyon Drive de-
tained the firemen for nearly four minutes. Those
minutes were critical, and on their arrival, they
discovered Cyrus Merton's burned body at his
front door. "He tried to escape," one of the firemen said, "but it was too late."

I always thought those words should have
been engraved on his tombstone.

11

~ Some years ago, in a neighborhood restaurant, I noticed a couple I knew to be married twenty years. They were seated close together in a booth, talking animatedly and holding hands. This unusual and reassuring sight set me thinking of another couple, a film producer and his wife who lived high above Los Angeles on Mulholland Drive and maintained a New York pied-à-terre on Central Park South.

She had a personal trainer, a closet full of Henry Lehr jumpsuits, and a private income. He had motorcycle dates with Sylvester Stallone and a producing career that generated several respected failures. "Don't you get tired of making films,"

Stallone once asked him, "that everyone talks about but nobody goes to?"

They were the embodiment of hip domestic bliss if ever I saw it, unencumbered by children or fear of the future or any apparent ambivalence. But because things happen, they later divorced. When I next encountered him, five years had gone by and he was living alone in the Los Angeles house they had shared. And he had stocked one closet of this house with jumpsuits in assorted colors, sizes four to eight, inferior copies of those once worn by his former wife. He offered these jumpsuits as a sort of party favor to the young women who visited his home and stayed the night.

Because things happen, I once attended a New Year's Eve gathering at the East Side apartment of a couple whose marriage had been disintegrating for some time. Still, the evening was congenial enough, with many guests, a potato-and-Gruyère casserole from *The Greens Cookbook*, and Miss Grace's lemon cake.

The following year, I attended the same party,

with the same host, same setting, similar food, same guests. Only one thing was different, and that was the wife.

The most curious aspect of this particular rendition of musical chairs was that it no longer seemed unusual. Everyone knew that things happen and that a consequence of this was marriages that dead-end, leading to the forfeiture of houses on Fire Island or the Vineyard and the more serious forfeiture of faith in plans and solemn vows.

These were insupportable things. Yet people lived with them. They lived with them because in a world where things happen and cannot be undone, there is no other choice.

12

~ It was easy to see why mid-life's first casualty was faith in the future and why, once gone, it was difficult to retrieve. I knew, for example, a woman who came to believe, in her late forties, that nothing she did could compensate for what she perceived as a fundamental loss of viability.

Previously, she had dyed her hair; with this depression, she stopped dyeing it. Soon, the lower portion of her hair was chestnut-brown while the top portion was mousy gray. And in that divide between gray and brown, you could see the point where hope expired.

I had a hard time with hope myself, and becoming older made it no easier, not for me or for anybody else. Take the journalist, a former wunderkind who never rebounded from having become too old to be precocious, and who fell into despondency when the young editor of *The New Republic*, Andrew Sullivan, attained a late twentieth-century emblem of arrival by appearing in a Gap ad. The writer's depression was directly attributable to concerns his former wife described as "age specific." And such concerns were pandemic among middle-aged men and women who spent their youths trying to prove they were as good as anyone and were disappointed either because they failed to prove it or because they proved it and then were condemned to spend the rest of their lives trying to top themselves.

In this world, well-received novelists could not match early work, aspiring novelists wrote screenplays, screenwriters wrote for television, and television writers worked in advertising.

It was as if, no matter what you aimed for, you probably aimed too high. There was nothing wrong with that; the striving was admirable. The terrible part was the ways in which people made their peace with it. "At least it's some recognition," I was once told by a film critic—who re-garded himself as a genius—on the eve of his receiving an award from the press association of Atlantic City.

All stories end one way or another, and mid-life affirmed how little relation there often was between the opening chapters and the denoue-ment. I took to imagining life as a script, with the words *cut to* at the conclusion of each scene. The principal benefit of this discipline was that it dis-pensed with envy, an emotion difficult to muster when you are convinced that the salient feature of good fortune is the rapidity with which it can change.

A useful parable in this regard concerned a handsome couple whose springtime wedding was a young girl's dream, replete with a waist-length veil composed of layers of tulle and lilies of the valley, four lovely bridesmaids, and a Vera Wang wedding gown. Cut to three months later, when the bride and her husband attended a party at which he flirted with one of her bridesmaids. Cut to the quarrel that ensued at two that morning, when the bride awakened her husband because she wanted, as she later told the arresting officers, "to work on our marriage."

Cut to a verbal battle, then a physical one; cut to the bridegroom's subsequent arrest, followed by a speedy divorce.

"I thought they would live happily ever after," one of their friends said later. Even in this envious world, the pristine visions of childhood are apt to die hard.

A life story was a case history. And unusual perceptive powers were not required to note cases in which ambition gave way to idleness, as with the writer, widely envied for his trust fund, who spent thirty years working fitfully on the same novel, never completing it, generating income by leasing out the main house while he and his family occupied the guest cottage. Then there was the White House correspondent whose career began during Watergate, when he was a fearless crusader for truth, justice, and his own advancement. But passing years had ensnared him in the same presumptive sense of privilege he had once taken such pleasure in deriding. "We in the White House press corps are the princes of journalism," he informed me after covering President Bush's first NATO conference.

I often thought of another television reporter, with whom I spent time in the late sixties when his marriage was unraveling. A year after we met, he took his disconsolate wife and three young children to Copenhagen, where he planned to find himself or be reassigned to Moscow, whichever happened first. Neither happened. He stayed on in Copenhagen, wondering what all disaffected people wonder in mid-life, which is whether the blemished past is a blueprint for the future. "Are you someone I could live with?" he wrote me. "Could I ever change?"

My answer was yes. I was twenty-four at the time. It would be a while before I understood what it means to make the same mistakes so often that you lose all faith in your ability to do things differently.

Still, even when I reached that stage, the gloom that was its consequence could still be pierced with the bright light cast by the occasional Happy Ending.

"You never know what will happen," I was told in a Madison Avenue hair salon by a fortyish woman who was having her honey-brown hair brightened with caramel streaks. "I marry this guy, he had nothing, and he ends up completely successful in menswear."

13

~ Just prior to my thirty-fifth birthday, I began to notice that my friends and I were conversing less about frivolous matters like love and work and more about true essentials like medical insurance and desk chairs with added support for the lower back. I enjoyed these dialogues. There was a sweetness to indulging in the same concerns and complaints I'd heard my mother and her friends express. In that sense, those early forays into the realm of mid-life were pleasantly regressive, a middle-aged version of tea party.

For, at first, mid-life really *did* seem like a game, one that you could choose to play or not, as if aging afflicted only those so foolish as to admit to growing older and could be avoided by anyone lucid enough to invoke the Satchel Paige line: "How old would you be if you didn't know how old you are?"

Yet the graver aspect of it all was never far away. And it manifested in a subtle attitudinal shift that converted a world where possibility once seemed limitless into a place where possibility seemed diminished. This signaled that the grief and dejection attending mid-life had set in, and once I detected these feelings in my own existence, I realized that I had seen them at work, for years, in other people's lives without comprehending what I was seeing.

When I first came upon them, I was still in my early twenties, working as a secretary for a theater producer. In this environment, life's payoffs could elude even demonically ambitious and hardworking people, who eventually deployed their energies in the service of despising everyone who fared better.

In the theater, I met people who were seriously baffled by an incapacity to parlay early success into something more substantial: actresses who yearned to be the next Katharine Hepburn but settled for minor roles in daytime soap operas; ballet dancers who retired after marrying men with vague pasts who chain-smoked Gauloises, wore slouch pants, and were always on the phone to presenters in Italy. For the lucky ones, disappointment was offset by secret relief that they no longer had to try so hard. For them, mid-life was a time to relax, and survival meant knowing when to cut one's losses.

Yet, at the same time, there would be the people for whom it all seemed to work out, whose faces could be seen beaming from the four-color pages of Sunday supplements, accompanying the article in which they affirmed that their every dream had come to pass. They were chimeras for other dreamers. And as years went by, aging hopefuls would recount auditioning for *The Lords of Flatbush* with an unknown actor named Sylvester Stallone, or rooming at the Manhattan Club on the floor below an aspiring actress named Diane Hall, who later changed her name to Diane Keaton.

The invariable point of these reminiscences was that the blessed, prior to their ascension, seemed as ordinary as you and I. If they could do it, ran the implication, you could do it. This was not necessarily true. But then, a cheering thought need not be true to make people feel better.

~ In 1969, I preserved a Library of Congress card in a gold frame with a green velvet matte. This card is number FI A 78-762 and is the entry for a project described on the card as "22 min. sd. b&w 16 mm. Summary: An art film and contemporary mood study."

At that time, I lived with the man who wrote and directed this twenty-two-minute black-and-white picture. He had long been saddled with the American albatross of Early Promise, and vanity about his potential, if not exactly burgeoning, status as an up-and-coming American director encouraged him to costume himself for the part in a black turtleneck, impenetrable sunglasses, and a meerschaum pipe. With the same notions of self in mind, he maintained a presence in certain cafés, where pitchers of sangria were consumed while he held forth on the auteur theory, the advantages of shooting in sixteen-millimeter black and white, and Truffaut's use of Jean-Pierre Leaud as an alter ego. Even in the late sixties, this sort of dialogue was miserably clichéd, but to know this, you had to be more sophisticated than I was.

We were an archetypal couple of the era, as you may agree when I tell you that moving in to-gether graced our household with two copies of every record cut by Bob Dylan and the Beatles, two copies of Mao's *Little Red Book*, two copies of Frantz Fanon's *Wretched of the Earth*, two hashish pipes, two batik bedspreads, two round oak tables with claw feet, and two Sister Corita posters.

To further establish those sixties credentials, the walls of our walk-up apartment were painted semigloss chocolate-brown and hung with ab-stract-expressionist canvases painted by his former wife. And this former wife was not merely a painter but also an actress and the star of his rather brief though extraordinarily insightful and much-praised art film and contemporary mood study, for which he had yet to find a distributor.

These were years when everyone was desperate to "relate," through folk songs composed on secondhand Martins or modern dance in the manner of the Judson Church or free-form verse in the manner of e. e. cummings or Ferlinghetti. In this fevered milieu, failure to find a distributor was widespread and fraught with metaphorical significance.

"It wasn't exactly what I had in mind," I recently heard a young woman say. She was referring to plans for a particular Friday evening, but her words could serve as an epitaph for a substantial portion of people in mid-life, including the filmmaker in the black turtleneck sweater.

As it happens, he and I parted not long after the sixties ended, and a few years later, I moved out of the apartment with the chocolate-brown walls and my sister moved in and painted the walls white. I did not hear from him for many years, but then he called and we met in a little bar off the boardwalk in Venice, California. He himself was in mid-life by then. There had been a marriage, a child he couldn't support, a divorce. He had long since stopped making films and begun taking saxophone lessons. It wasn't exactly what he had in mind, but I seemed to be the only one to know it.

∽ I was in my late twenties when work brought me to Los Angeles, where youth has always been the best card to play and which proved, therefore, a useful place for viewing mid-life's early effects. Los Angeles was filled with people who were too restless and ambitious to remain in the South or the East or the Midwest. These people tended to wear their wristwatches in bed, bring their date-books to the beach, refer to vacations as "unstructured time," and, in many cases, to rely on an excess of energy to compensate for a glaring absence of talent or luck.

Newcomers had a certain brazenness, the conviction that *it* would take place, that they would sell the screenplay in which interest had recently been expressed by someone who once worked with John Schlesinger or that they would receive that career-making callback from a casting director scouting for Francis Ford Coppola.

As time passed, some achieved their stated goal of becoming rich and famous. Others enrolled in law school or opened a shop in Malibu where they sold Navajo rugs and Hopi baskets. Still others kept trying to succeed, in the absence of evidence that this was prudent, their sense of well-being increasingly at the mercy of any unemployed actor waiting on tables in a studio commissary who failed to treat them as they dreamed of being treated.

Years later, you would see them, and they would not quite meet your eye, and for people whose favorite topic had always been themselves, they would display a marked lack of interest in detailing how they came to stand in for the second lead in a pilot that never became a series or to be the late-shift hostess at the Old World on Sunset or to sell vintage clothing in the San Fernando Valley.

Among the people I observed in Los Angeles was a man who had served as Bob Dylan's factotum in the glory days when there was nothing to regret and to be obnoxious was a job qualification.

"Are your nipples pink, or are they brown?" he asked a woman I knew five minutes into their first date. In those years, being in league with Dylan meant never having to say you're sorry.

As it turned out, this man was a gifted musician, too, though expending effort on his own behalf seems to have interested him less than tending to Dylan. In the early eighties, I saw him perform at McCabe's Guitar Shop on Pico Boulevard, a venue for folkies who'd known better days. He was very good, and judging from several songs he wrote, it seemed he'd come to regret having bartered away his early potential to be the second-coolest man in the music business.

Yet no case of misspent promise seemed more poignant than that of Colonel Edwin E. "Buzz" Aldrin, with whom I spent time eight years after he became the second man to set foot on the moon, an honor so fleeting that "Who was Buzz Aldrin?" later became the answer to a *Jeopardy* question.

We met at a press conference convened to announce his recent recovery from alcoholism.

"When you returned from the moon," a reporter asked him, "did you feel that your life had reached its pinnacle, that there were no challenges to greet you, no oceans to cross, no mountains to climb?"

The colonel had frightened blue eyes. But he could muster a hero's dignity. "Yes," he said.

In those days, Colonel Aldrin was in his late forties, drifting, uncentered. He had a part-time job selling cars, early retirement from the Air Force having deprived him of his principal area of competence. Now he was left to display his *Apollo 11* ring to strangers, to drive too fast in a Honda with a bumper sticker that proclaimed Divers Do It Deeper, and to spend evenings at home with his model planetarium, seated on the couch of his darkened ground-floor apartment, pointing out the stars with an illuminated arrow.

A divided man, gruff and sweet, pompous and unsure, he had devolved into an honored guest at ceremonial functions, the kind of American celebrity whose future lies chiefly in game shows and product endorsements and in being fawned over by anyone who continued to perceive in him an opportunity to make a dollar.

On hand for returning Apollo flights or seated in the reviewing stand when the space shuttle touched down, he would look around with the furtiveness common to people who have been celebrated and renowned and who want to see if anyone remembers them.

Buzz Aldrin was unhappy because he had to live with the knowledge that his best days were behind him. In fact, many people live that way, especially the ones who figure out that the proverbial fifteen minutes of fame are never enough.

When Buzz Aldrin had his fifteen minutes, the avenues of the world stood empty as citizens of every nation were transfixed by the televised vision of two creatures who seemed neither man nor machine gamboling on the moon. They had jumped and danced and then returned to earth, where they were met with cheers and motorcades and hailstorms of confetti, and they could be forgiven if, in those days, they failed to remember that many are granted some time in the sun, and then their time ends and it is someone else's time.

Over the years, I lost track of Buzz Aldrin, though after I moved to New York, I occasionally heard things about him. I heard he remarried. I heard he had a face-lift. I heard he participated in CNN's tribute to the twenty-fifth anniversary of the moon landing. But I never heard whether he made peace with the fact that life could never provide him another occasion like those moments when he danced on the moon and the entire world stopped what it was doing to watch him dance.

~ The deduction to be derived from these real-life scenarios was that getting stuck is distinctly possible, that you could become as incapable of going forward as you were of going back. This was a common condition, though survivors knew that to dwell on it was pointless. There was a peculiar heroism in that, the curious, last-ditch heroism of unhappy people who recognize that their final chance depends on the ability to ignore their own misery.

14

~ Because I was having trouble with the middle, I wanted to return to the start. So one day I took the eight o'clock train from New York to Philadelphia, then boarded a second train heading north from Suburban Station to the town where I was raised.

I had been warned that when you go home, everything seems shabbier and less imposing than you remember. It was true. The two-story fieldstone house where my family once lived turned out to be set on a tiny knoll that I remember as a noble hill. The Japanese cherry tree in the front yard, whose pink blossoms blanketed the lawn in spring, was not, as memory insisted, particularly tall. The backyard oak tree was reduced to a stump. The wooden swing and sliding board were gone. But there was still the Donley-Bonner Package Receiver, where the milkman deposited glass bottles of milk, skimmed on the bottom and topped with cream. Similar bottles have since become available in markets, American nostalgia purveyed twenty-four hours a day at the Food Emporium.

As a rule, I do not feel old, but I felt old that day, and each step I took felt heavy on the gray-white pavements bordered with late-blooming asters, where I once rode my tricycle and drew hopscotch grids in pink chalk.

Across from my family's home was the three-story Victorian house belonging to the Jennings family. Mrs. Jennings took in sewing. In her back parlor, my two small sisters and I had our dresses shortened while we pleaded in vain for the longer hemlines that grown-up women wore.

When I last saw Mr. and Mrs. Jennings, they were a robust pair, well-fed people in their late forties, skin reddened from tending tulips and mowing the lawn. But when a dusty gray Chevrolet turned into their driveway, I saw Mr. Jennings for the first time in thirty years. He had grown thin and he moved slowly. His car had a license plate with a wheelchair symbol.

I had left the Jennings' neighborhood when I was sixteen and no better equipped to handle the future than anyone else. I did not know then that nothing gold can stay or that things happen and cannot be undone or that it is possible to reach a stage at which the essential question shifts from how much you can expect to how much you can endure.

Mr. Jennings caught my eye. He stared at me, his face wary and pinched.

"I used to live across the street," I told him.

"Oh, right," he said finally. "Well, how've you been?"

"Oh, just fine," I said. "And you?"

15

~ Mid-life's initial stages are accompanied by a myopia that obstructs awareness of what you have gained and permits you to see only loss. Later, you discover that gains were accruing all along, like interest in a bank account you forgot you had. At least, that is how it was for me, and complicating this condition is that mid-life is filled with genuine loss, each jarring, some as shocking as death, others as predictable as finding you have ceased to be the prettiest girl at the party.

The grief generated by these losses eventually recedes, but until it does, they make for a troubled time.

～ The first loss of my particular mid-life was of a two-year-old love affair. I was no good at endings, and in the months before this one took place, I would drive home in the evenings, pretend I was on my way to an empty apartment, and try to imagine how that made me feel. It made me feel terrible.

During those weeks, I discovered I was pregnant. Initially, it seemed reasonable to have the baby and raise it by myself. I did not want to accept, at first, that in a situation as unsettled as mine, this might not be a good idea.

I was thirty-seven years old. My doctor warned that it could be my last chance to have a child. I didn't believe him, because I still believed that opportunity is infinite.

～ On the afternoon of what was called the procedure a friend drove me to a tidy three-story building overlooking the Marina on Admiralty

Way. This was abortion California-style, with a complimentary ten-milligram Valium and the ceiling above the operating table decked out with spray-painted clouds and a sign that read Be Calm. I was calm. And afterward, my friend and I drove to the coffee bar at Charmer's Market, ate poached salmon, and talked about how men help you into problems and women help you out of them, a conversation typical of the era.

That was the end of it, and I did not allow myself to think any more about it because thinking about it would make me feel worse. When you need to get by, you try not to do things that make you feel worse.

Two weeks later, I was living alone again. After that, I would stand at my window late at night, watching cars proceed south along Neilson Way, their red lights fading into the far distance as they sped toward Venice Beach through the dark-gray mesh of fog that floats in from the ocean. Each car seemed a warning that life was passing me by. On certain nights I watched the cars for a very long time.

∼ People who fear the future tend to ruminate about the past. The more fearful of the future I became, the more I found myself sifting through faded family photographs and letters.

One photograph that especially absorbed me was a black-and-white snapshot of my father and me, taken on a visit to the zoo when I was small.

We are standing in front of a moose. My father is looking up at the moose. I am looking up at my father. He was about thirty then and must have seemed very big and wondrous to me, because that's what you see in my expression.

Eight years after this picture was taken, my parents divorced. They made lasting marriages with other people. After that, there were visits with my father, gifts on holidays, letters I always saved. But there are constraints on a relationship with any parent, particularly one with whom you have not lived since you were eleven. By the time I reached mid-life, I had become accustomed to seeing him just a few times a year, and on each of those occasions, he would say something clever or wise, and his words invariably charmed me and left me wishing I had known him better.

In that photograph of my father and me, I hoped to find a relatedness between the segments of my life that comprised its *then* and *now*. In light of the uncertainty around me, a link like that might have been consoling. But when it proved elusive, those faded family photographs simply became further evidence of loss.

∼ In those first months of my mid-life, I felt empty and flat, and in an effort to combat this, I got in the habit of going for a run. I would run along the dull, white sidewalks of my tidy neighborhood, where litter dared not fall, passing vignettes of what I perceived as normal life. I'd run past children being bundled off to school, past fathers on their way to work, past mothers going off to jobs or returning from the market with brown paper bags brimming with family-size boxes of detergent or cereal. I liked observing people whose lives seemed to be conducted so purposefully.

But then, I must have seemed purposeful, too, striding down their pavements, following my daily route, a three-mile circle. To run in a circle while so much of living moved quietly by was yet another aspect of my life that struck me as metaphorical.

It was not that my existence was dismal. But lives, like mountains, have a way of seeming more impressive from a distance. From a distance, there was the fellowship from a foundation in the East, the articles in magazines and on editorial pages, each laden with the declarative sentences of a woman whose beliefs and identity seemed, if anything, more fixed and certain than good reason could allow.

This assured individual filled in Surface Passenger Surveys handed out on city buses, voted in off-year elections, sent Christmastime contributions to Cancer Care and Meals-on-Wheels, and appeared to be a civic-minded person who had assumed her place in the world.

But at night, I would slip between the cool, soft sheets and lie there very still and very quiet, knowing that no one knew where I was or what I was doing. That same realization could exhilarate me during the day. But not at night.

Being alone had never troubled me. But I did not like it now, not because it was unbearable, but because of what it might portend.

I tried not to brood. I tried to be cheerful. At times I tried too hard. By the end of the day, I was often tired.

"Some of this loneliness is exhaustion," I wrote in my diary, "and some of this exhaustion is loneliness."

∽ For a number of months, I went to a cognitive therapist. I paid him to tell me what I could have deduced for myself: that one reason people become depressed is that they feed themselves depressing information. In mid-life, that information was apt to be that you never had what you wanted and never would, an equation whose most insidious aspect was the way it implied that the only things worth measuring your life by are things you do not possess.

In this regard, I was chastened by a cautionary tale concerning my grandmother's sister, whose dashing husband wore ascots, bred horses, and took her to Paris for their honeymoon. During their first stroll down the Champs-Elysées, she noticed a pair of high-heeled shoes in a shop window. She asked him to buy them for her. He refused. She had enough shoes, he said. She persisted. He refused again, this time adamantly. And so she gleaned that this marriage, contrary to expectation, would not fulfill her every desire.

She never got over it. She never forgave what it implied. From then on, she was shrouded in anger, and eventually he turned to more pliant, forgiving women, and before long her bitterness extended far beyond the margins of being denied any particular object. Into each life an unobtainable pair of shoes must fall, and it had finally occurred to me that one of life's essential tasks is adjusting to not getting them.

16

~ In the earliest phase of my mid-life depression, I subscribed to the simple, mechanistic notion that a moving target is harder to hit. If nothing gold could stay, then I was not about to stay either, not anywhere, at least not for longer than absolutely necessary. I worked many hours each day, but my work was eminently portable, permitting me to offer myself for house-sitting duty on both coasts to friends whose homes stood empty while they judged a ballet contest in Mississippi or accompanied their husband to a physicist's conference in Baltimore or did wardrobe for Linda Evans on a Movie of the Week.

They would leave keys in the bike shed or the outdoor grill, while inside, on the kitchen counter, would be written reminders to close the garage door, to turn the heat to 60 at night, to feed the cat, to water the newly planted moonvines. It was a relief to enter an empty house where there was every practical item I required, the bath towels and bed sheets and dish soap of daily life, combined with the silent unreality of a stage set.

After these respites, I returned to Los Angeles, where the much ballyhooed concept of Looking Out for Number One had raised unabashed solipsism to a virtue, and where I moved to a ground-floor room at the St. Regis Motor Hotel when my apartment was engulfed by mudslides because a neighbor had neglected to grant an easement for replacement of a storm drain.

In Los Angeles, it seemed that a sizable portion of the male population was writing magazine features or breaking news stories or movie scripts that often were optioned but rarely were made. These men were so dominated by the anxiety to locate that life-altering Good Story that they failed to note their own featured role in one of the more engaging true-life sagas, in which good-looking thirtyish women with José Eber haircuts and mid-level production jobs lunched with men like them at Ma Maison or La Serre. These occasions tended to have a subterranean purpose that had nothing to do with pitching stories or second-draft revisions or distribution rights worldwide. Rather, they supplied the women with opportunities to parlay evident charms before it was too late, offering them in exchange for Tiffany engagement rings and suites at the Carlyle in New York while fitting a wedding dress with Carolina Herrera.

For these women intended to enter mid-life with that particular set of things prized by individuals who aspire to a north-of-Sunset address: the country kitchen floored in Portuguese tiles, the garden bordered with scarlet bougainvillea, the German masseuse with wonderful hands, the unlisted home number of their hair colorist, the useful bits of folk wisdom shared with them by their handsome Hispanic poolman, the husband whose efficient but not unduly good-looking secretary reminded him to send red velvet roses on Valentine's Day.

Then there were women like me, which is to say, unattached women who spent evenings with similarly situated females during which it was not unheard of for someone to wonder whether hemorrhoid cream really could be used to tighten lines around the eyes. If I had five lives, I used to think, this particular Los Angeles existence would have been reasonable enough for one of them. But it was insufficiently rewarding for a person who planned to live just once.

One day, an editor at *Life* magazine called and asked if I wanted to come to New York to do a piece about the making of the movie *The Pope of Greenwich Village*, whose star was a twenty-seven-year-old actor named Mickey Rourke, then being touted as the Marlon Brando of the eighties, a comparison that would later be regarded as inflated.

His costar was Eric Roberts, one of the more gifted young actors working at that time. But the determining factor in a career is not simply talent, and Eric Roberts, a troubled young man whose troubles came across on-screen, never—in Hollywood parlance—really happened. So while I was supposed to be writing about film stars of the future, the piece I eventually wrote is of interest only for the way it demonstrates that the future is not easy to foresee and for an accompanying photograph of the presumably up-and-coming Eric Roberts at home with his younger sister, an unknown actress named Julia Roberts. What I am saying is that it is rarely clear where things are tending.

In any case, after that call came from *Life* magazine, I never admitted I was moving from Los Angeles, not even to myself. Instead, in that curiously de facto way major decisions are often made, I took out three suitcases and packed, for what was to be a week in New York at the end of September, most of my wardrobe and all my winter clothes.

The next evening, I checked into the Mayflower Hotel at the southwest edge of Central Park, where an on-arrival message informed me that the commissioning studio had determined they need not pay the back-end money on a script I had recently written that had more recently been put into turnaround. This arcane sequence of events meant that I was broke. And so I stayed on at the Mayflower, stretching what should have been seven days of reporting about what was, at best, a minor picture into ten days, then fourteen, then more, because as long as I kept reporting, *Life* magazine would pay my way, and having your way paid is essential when you do not have money enough to vacate room 1412 of the Mayflower.

After shooting wrapped each night, I would go to the Mayflower bar, where there were platters of free crudités, bowls of curried-yogurt dip, and Mickey Rourke. Rourke was always encircled by younger actors like Matt Dillon and Sean Penn, and by a cadre of middle-aged men who had longed to be contenders. Now that it seemed un-likely that this ambition would be gratified, they had attached themselves to Rourke, attempting to garner some sense of meaning and distinction by laughing loudly at his jokes, fetching his shortwave radio from his suite when he wanted to listen to jazz on a park bench at two A.M., and being atten-tive while he detailed, for the third time that eve-ning, the whispered conversation he had had with another of his costars, Daryl Hannah. These men had assumed the role of trusted gofer, a part someone was always playing in the presence of Hollywood actors. It had its perks, though it was, essentially, a demeaning role that became considerably more demeaning when the star was twenty-five years younger than the gofers.

Not that the gofers seemed bothered by this, but it bothered me, because I was becoming attuned to the way that age puts a different spin on things. Getting stuck in room 1412 of the Mayflower, for example, could be an amusing adventure when you are eighteen, but at thirty-eight, it could only be a sign of impending failure.

One day I woke up at the Mayflower and felt very strange. I did not know why. It was the middle of October. Then I remembered that this was the week the baby I aborted was due to be born.

~ In the days that followed, I avoided stepping on cracks in the pavement. I couldn't buy a king-size tube of toothpaste because it set me thinking about the dreadful things that could happen before the toothpaste was used up. The rootlessness of hotel life was so unsettling that I moved to the Greenwich Village apartment of a friend who was out of town. But once there, I couldn't sleep and instead walked the deserted Village streets in those desolate hours when it is too late to call anyone in Los Angeles and too early to call anyone in New York. Finally, I went back to the Mayflower, where I slept in my clothes each night with the television on.

When it came time for Thanksgiving, I went with Mickey Rourke and his minions to what he had been told was a party at the home of the film producer Robert Evans. It turned out to be precisely that: a party at the home of Robert Evans. The presumed host—touted in his charmed and enviable youth as a new Irving Thalberg though fallen in recent years on less-fruitful times—was neither in attendance nor, as it turned out, involved in the remotest way with the evening's guest list.

Who did the inviting for this Gatsbyesque affair was a matter destined to remain forever vague. All that was certain was that Matt Dillon turned up because he was told that Mickey Rourke would be attending, while Rourke turned up because he was told Matt Dillon would be there. It made for a curious evening, complete with a presliced thirty-pound cold turkey studded with orange slices and maraschino cherries from Wolfs Delicatessen on Sixth Avenue, and the subtle seductions playing out between undiscovered ingenues and middle-aged set designers and cinematographers of a certain renown whose wives were either conveniently at home or busy on other pictures that had left them stranded on location.

A decade or so later, as I write this, one of those cinematographers has become a director, and Robert Evans, after publishing a gossip-laden autobiography that seemed to be an endmost effort to resuscitate a moribund career, is again producing movies and developing one called *Jimmy the Rumor* with Mickey Rourke, which is, Rourke recently told a reporter, "about a bastard born in a mailbox."

Rourke is likewise planning a comeback after a decade of demonstrating that his salient talents are for boxing, stirring up trouble, and allegedly abusing his wife. And his gofers, in the meanwhile, denied reports that Rourke's stay in an Italian hospital was occasioned by a suicide attempt.

But that night, it was clear only that this was a Thanksgiving for disaffected people. And here again, it made a difference whether you were in mid-life or not. Younger people seemed perfectly at ease. But anyone over thirty-five looked bemused and injured while they helped themselves to the Stoli of the absent host, as if secretly wondering if this was all there was.

～ That was the Thanksgiving of 1983. The following day, a friend introduced me to a lanky man with dark, bright eyes. This man was a writer, too, and we smiled at each other, and it was one of those classic instances of delusion at first sight, in the course of which we each saw enough in the other's smile to spend the next several years trying to de-emphasize the differences between us.

He was not, in any respect, like so many men I had met in California: He did not wear a gold chain, did not seem particularly driven by money or power, did not spend evenings speculating as to why his agent failed to call, did not glaze over at the start of any conversation not about himself.

He lived in the Village, on Sullivan Street, in an airy fourth-floor walk-up, where he had installed shelves from the floor to the ceiling and packed them with books, records, and musical instruments. I loved the way he could become mesmerized when he played his Gibson guitar or listened to Solti's recording of Wagner's *Parsifal* or to scratchy old 78s of Bob Wills and His Texas Playboys.

Most love affairs, however complex, have a single founding point, and this affinity for music was ours. I did not know then that he had something of the musician's facility for using music to obliterate what he did not wish to deal with or that his unqualified passion for all types of music would eventually produce in me a craving for silence. But we are talking about the beginning here, not about the end.

Six months later, we were married. I cut into our wedding cake and discovered it was stale. This bothered me for obvious reasons, and because I believe in omens.

17

~ When I was small, I spent weekends with my grandparents. My grandfather had begun life as one of five sons of an indigent tailor from Kiev and went on to establish one of the largest men's clothing businesses in the world. But he was one of those men so driven to achieve that they never quite believe they have arrived. His success did surprisingly little to reassure him, though he attempted to obscure this, for he was the product of a belief system in which women were expected to be dependent and men were expected to be strong. As a consequence, his shyness and discomfort were concealed behind a barrage of puns and jokes, while his anxieties about being needed were assuaged by the generous tips he left on restaurant tables, the good jewelry he selected for his daughter and his wife, the shiny half-dollar pieces he gave his nieces and granddaughters at frequent intervals.

On Sundays, we went to his country club, and late in the day, he would disappear into the big room behind a massive oak door where men played gin rummy, drank whiskey, and smoked thick Cuban cigars. He would open the door and be enveloped by that haze of smoke with sunlight straining through it. It seemed forbidden and bewitching and unearthly, and I was convinced, when I was small, that heaven is a smoke-filled room.

My grandfather played cards until dinnertime, when I was dispatched to fetch him to the table. I would stand on tiptoe and knock on the massive oak door with the flat of my hand. When the door was opened, I would ask, "Is my grandfather in there?" He was always there, and each time he appeared in the doorway, I felt protected.

When I was knocking on that oak door, my

grandfather was approximately the age I am now. He had entered his own mid-life having fulfilled the immigrant's dream, but then he overreached during the boom of the late sixties and lost everything he had. And so he became acquainted with another fact that has a way of becoming relevant in mid-life, namely, that anything you struggle to achieve can be snatched away.

He was in his seventies by then, old enough to recognize that the difference between those who prevail and those who do not is the willingness to keep on. He kept on. He took out three bank loans and opened a store in Passaic, New Jersey, the size of three football fields, in which he carried slightly damaged goods.

For the next twelve years, he boarded the seven A.M. train from Philadelphia to Newark, then spent the day walking the floor of his store, making his jokes and puns and slipping Snickers bars and Mason Mints into the hands of the customers to whom he sold irregular shirts and suits and two-dollar ties. "This saved my life," he once told me.

It was a far distance from three-course lunches at the best tables at "21" and the suite of offices overlooking Manhattan, where his private closet was accessorized with brass fittings and lined with alligator skin. But he was a survivor, and among his kind, the simple act of surviving matters more than what you do to survive.

When he was eighty-six, he had a mild stroke. "The only strokes I have are on the golf course," he told the doctor. But that was bravado. Weeks later, he retired, once again in the name of survival. After that, playing cards and smoking cigars with other men were upgraded from an active man's Sunday relaxation to vestiges of another life, another time, and to being among the few things he still did.

"Your grandfather's dying to say hello," my grandmother told me when I called one evening.

"I'm living to say hello," said my grandfather. It was meant to be another of his little jokes, but so much had gone from his life by then that I think he may have meant it.

∿ One Monday morning, my grandfather woke at eight and dressed in a blue shirt and freshly pressed gray slacks. He draped a navy-blue blazer over the wooden hanger of the silent valet in his room. After that, he must have opened his dresser drawer, selected a crimson silk pocket scarf, folded it into neat quarters, and placed it in the breast pocket of his blazer.

"What's for breakfast?" he asked my grand-mother.

"Oatmeal," she told him.

"Good," he replied. As far as anyone knows, that was the last thing he ever said.

My grandmother was old by then, and the simplest tasks were becoming a challenge. By the time she got the oatmeal cooked, spooned it into the white china breakfast bowl, and placed that bowl on the table, the momentous had once again intruded on the ordinary, and my grandfather had been dead five minutes.

Eighteen hours later, I was lying beside the

older of my two sisters in the twin beds of our grandfather's room, where the silent valet was still draped with the blue blazer brightened by that crimson pocket scarf.

For years prior to that evening, I had steeled myself whenever the phone rang after ten at night in case it would bring news that my grandfather was dead. His health was perfect. He had no maladies or complaints. It was simply that I was determined to be prepared. But when that call came, it was ten in the morning and I was not prepared at all. Generally speaking, being prepared is not an option in life, no matter what you determine.

∽ Two days later, my mother and I arrived at my grandfather's viewing. The chapel door was closed. It was the only viewing of the day. The funeral home was silent and empty. They were not ready for us, so we took a walk, proceeding slowly hand in hand along crowded city streets.

That early winter morning my mother and I were, respectively, ages sixty-five and forty-two,

two adult women who never quite located, in their relation to one another, the balance between too much closeness and too much distance. Yet in recent years, we had made peace at last, in the process proving that you don't have to work something out in order to resolve it. Now we had been brought closer still by the death of the man who taught us both that family is your custodian.

By the time we returned, loudspeakers were piping a cassette tape of the Allegretto from Beethoven's Seventh Symphony into the lobby, where someone had placed three oversize sprays of browning white carnations left over from another funeral.

The undertaker stood before the chapel door, his phlegmatic features subdued in an expression he must have deemed appropriately somber. I remember that he beckoned to us. And with that gesture, the scene assumed its own weird momentum, like a Fellini film enacted underwater.

I remember looking at the chapel door. And I remember what I said: "Is my grandfather in there?"

And I remember thinking, as I spoke those familiar words, that there would be no earthly reason to ever say them again.

∼ Since that day, I have often passed places that remind me of my grandfather: Madison Square Garden, where we saw a closed-circuit screening of the third Ali-Frazier fight; the Sherry-Netherland Hotel on Fifth Avenue, where he and my grandmother often stayed. These places always evoke in me something he used to say. He used to say, "You'll never have to worry."

And though I certainly managed to worry, I can also relay that just as I felt protected while my grandfather was alive, once he was gone, something went from my life that would never be replaced. For after my grandfather died, I never felt as protected again.

But then, I was in mid-life and just beginning to understand that every person is alone in the ways that matter most.

18

~ "Thanks for taking care of her," my grandfather once told my husband. "We appreciate it."

For reasons having nothing to do with my grandfather's death but following on the heels of it, my husband and I, after four years of marriage, began taking less good care of each other.

"I appreciate it," I would imagine saying to him, with as much sarcasm as I would be able to summon, when he left town on the weekend of my birthday to play his banjo at a square dance. And I would hope he would forget to call. I would be angry if he forgot my birthday, but if he remembered, I would be angry, too, because that would deprive me of my excuse for being angry.

I kept thinking of a conversation I had, shortly

before our wedding, with an editor whose five-year marriage was falling apart, a misfortune convincing him that weariness with your partner's anxieties, pretensions, and complaints can make you feel irritated by the very sight of the person who once seemed the best thing that ever happened to you.

He had detailed the myriad ways you can cease paying attention to someone whose dependence you once encouraged, and I tried not to seem appalled by his confession of chronic intolerance and self-absorption.

These were the staples of every unhappy alliance, though it was reasonable to wonder which came first, the unhappiness or the behavior. In either case, the general custom was that first you sabotaged your marriage and then you sabotaged your self-regard by behaving in ways you swore you never would.

After that, there was apt to be upheaval or erosion. In our particular case, a marriage was destroyed in the absence of any momentous occurrence. There were no infidelities, no slammed doors, no drinks hurled in anyone's face, no screaming matches in restaurants or parks. Still, there are gradations and styles of bad behavior, and in our own way, each of us behaved badly.

I think he felt, as I did, that he was living with a person he did not know. Yet neither of us had changed. We had merely gone back to being the people we had been before, whose differing ideas about how to vote or act at a dinner party or spend Saturday afternoon had finally surfaced and then become, with sufficient repetition, different ideas about living a life. This was a familiar pattern, and when it occurred, it always seemed that the people had changed, and in a sense they had, though not because they were deceitful.

Of course, everyone is initially more generous and less needy than he will be later, which is why new relationships tend to come with ninety-day guarantees. That wonderful and perfect person you fell in love with is never quite the person you end up with, because falling in love is a transforming experience and anyone to whom it happens becomes happier and more lustrous than he is ordinarily. For in that early season of hope, it is common to believe that your new love will be different from the rest and that you will be different, too, that you will transcend the pettiness and self-concern that overwhelmed all previous affairs. Naturally, neither partner turns out to be as flawless as they seemed, and many find this inevitability impossible to forgive.

In my own marriage, the disappointment remained subdued. We simply drifted into that extreme politeness that, in an intimate relationship, can constitute the ultimate hostility. Though I could tell he was the same man who brought me daffodils in spring and wrote out the chords of "Devoted to You" when teaching me to play guitar, because I would hear him talking to the dog in that same dear and loving way he used to talk to me.

19

~ During the day, helpful advice to those in troubled marriages was frequently offered on the television program *Sonya Live*, hosted by Dr. Sonya Friedman, who happened to be a psychotherapist.

"Make sure you have a strategy," Sonya advised, "that will help you get what you want."

I had no such strategy but was open to suggestion. "Go see *Working Girl* if you're feeling victimized," suggested Sonya, though this did not seem quite to the point.

The particular point that preoccupied me was that so many marriages were troubled, that so many women spent sleepless nights beside dozing men who either were oblivious to their misery or unmoved by it.

"Nothing kills sex as quickly as resentment and boredom," a doctor from San Francisco told Sonya.

"What do you do about it?" Sonya asked brightly.

"Well, Sonya," said the doctor, "you have to talk about it."

This reasonable idea would not have helped my marriage. My husband and I often talked about such things only to discover that it is impossible to talk away resentment and boredom that have largely been engendered by too much talk about the marriage.

In the beginning, when we bought the country house, we speculated about the particular miseries besetting the previous tenant, a sullen, overweight woman of forty-five who kept four giant trash bags stuffed with paperback romances in the bedroom and snacked on the Surprise cakes she concocted from Duncan Hines yellow cake mix and canned fruit salad. I assumed her husband was, like many men, not reticent about placing his own needs first. And I came to wonder if she had been treated worse than other women or was simply less adept at dealing with the usual treatment. And I wondered if she remained in the marriage because she loved her husband or because she believed that, for a woman of her age, there weren't many moves left.

By the time I reached that age, my husband was spending every weekend in the country house where this woman had lived, while I remained in the city, trying to avoid the anxiety produced by the prospect of being alone again.

I worked eighteen-hour days. Work was my stay against dislocation. And it was not entirely coincidental that the stories interesting me most were domestic-violence cases like that of LouAnn Fratt, an upper-middle-class lady who went to the apartment of her estranged and wayward husband, murdered him with a kitchen knife, then took the bloody weapon home in her Gucci bag. I could appreciate the rage of LouAnn Fratt and of all the disappointed women for whom life does not work out as planned.

And I found myself contemplating the Lou-Ann Fratts of this world on solitary walks in Riverside Park, where it often seemed that everyone else was promenading arm-in-arm with their own true love.

On these walks, I hoped not to encounter anyone I knew, for my face increasingly conveyed the particular feelings that can overtake a woman in mid-life who believes there aren't many moves left.

20

~ When my husband was away, I spent time with my friend Jim. There were differences between Jim and my husband, chief among them that Jim was homosexual and seemed to enjoy my company.

Jim was thirty-two then, and he was a hairdresser. This was actually what he had set out to be—something of a rarity in New York, where dreams so often outpaced abilities and people planned careers as actresses or singers or abstract expressionists but earned their keep as waitresses or secretaries or hairstylists.

But Jim had wanted to cut hair, though he felt obliged to joke about his profession, as when he gave me a Harvard sweatshirt saying he got it while studying at the Harvard School of Beauty.

Like many people, Jim fared well with friends, from whom he expected relatively little, and considerably less well with lovers, from whom he expected a lot. When I knew him, he was embroiled in yet another troubled affair with a young man who was too self-concerned to accord him what he needed and deserved.

This young man was eventually diagnosed with AIDS and soon became gravely ill and entered St. Vincent's Hospital. Jim visited him there each morning, and the young man was stirred by the tenderness with which Jim held his hand and fed him, and they drew close as the days went by.

The young man spoke about things they would do when he recovered. Jim wanted him to acknowledge there would be no recovery. But the young man either couldn't or wouldn't, and this denial worried Jim, who had taken too much acid in his youth and liked to converse, providing the hour was sufficiently late, about the importance of completely experiencing death.

Then the young man died, and the following winter, Jim was diagnosed as HIV-positive. For some time after that, he was the one in denial.

～ That first winter of his illness, Jim stopped walking past the boutiques on Columbus Avenue, where he used to buy Ivy League shirts and Swatch watches. He walked through Central Park instead. He was not interested in clothes; he was interested in the way the lusterless winter sun reflected on the frozen pond, and the way icicles fastened upon the lakeside pagoda, and the way resolute squirrels hastened across the crusty snow.

When the thaw came, he looked for crocuses and other harbingers of spring, though by early summer he abandoned this Waldenesque mode, began walking Columbus Avenue again, and started buying furniture. He bought a Stickley table, a Mission couch and rocking chair with chocolate-brown leather cushions, three art-deco lamps, two Persian carpets, and countless pieces of Rosedale pottery. I think he was hoping to convince himself that a person with beautiful possessions such as these would have to be around to enjoy them.

"How could anyone die when there is so much shopping left to do?" he would say. He laughed when he said it, but he wasn't really kidding.

One year after his diagnosis, Jim gave in and signed the will that would disperse these belongings. That was the afternoon he was hospitalized and ceased being in denial. His apartment was twenty blocks from mine, and I walked there that late summer afternoon, stopping first at Wendy's to get him a vanilla milk shake, which had become the only sustenance he could manage, then making a second stop at Golden's stationery to buy him a premade will.

Soon after that day, he made the decision to die at home. Home was the two-room apartment he still kept in Minneapolis, one block from Lake of the Isle's, where he first lived on his own. He returned there in the fall, intent on living long enough to see another midwestern spring.

When I visited him in December, he did not always know who I was. To sit at his bedside was to glimpse someone caught at the endpoint known as dying, a province that is neither death nor life. Where Jim had gone, the loneliness was impenetrable and unassuagable.

"Are you afraid?" I asked.

"All the time," he said.

"Of the pain?"

"That," he said, "and that something will happen fast."

Jim weighed one hundred pounds. He could hardly walk. He could not lift his head from his chest. He seemed far past the point at which things happen fast.

But I suppose these things look different when you are the one who is dying.

∼ Jim had wanted to see one more spring, but the day he died, the ground was still covered with snow. I do not think this would have surprised him. Dying at thirty-four was surely all the proof he needed that what you want does not necessarily bear on what you get.

There was a time when I was genuinely surprised if someone was denied his "heart's desire," as significant yearnings are sometimes described.

But after Jim died, I was no longer capable of surprise, because to be surprised, you must place stock in the reliability of natural order.

I was twelve years older than Jim. He should have outlived me. But it had become common for people to arrange memorial services for the people who might have arranged those services for them if natural order still had meaning.

The inability to be surprised was an attribute of mid-life, too. After a certain point, if you are surprised, it can only mean you haven't been paying attention.

21

∼ One summer night, a year and a half after I was married, I went to dinner with some friends. These women were in their mid-thirties and absorbed by redesigning regional magazines or editing a series of articles about presidential candidates or finding a script that would interest Sydney Pollack. I had been as engrossed in work as they, but in those first months of marriage, the work that previously had been the central element in my existence suddenly and unexpectedly devolved into something I did for money.

And it was another of life's little ironies that I was more at ease than ever before, now that I resembled the sort of homebody I once resolutely avoided, to whom notable endeavor meant making a table from a weathered plank door and staking the Holland tomatoes. I had even begun to make white eyelet curtains and a rag doll in a blue-and-white-checked muslin dress for what might be a baby's room someday.

"You'll be the one to have children," one of the women told me that night, and everyone agreed. Though as things turned out, I never had a child, and each of them did.

But you would not have guessed, that dank summer night in Greenwich Village, that within a few years these women would relinquish the careers they spoke of with such commitment then and move with their families to Gramercy Park or Del Mar or the Maryland shore. But they did, and afterward they sent Polaroids of the baby, and I sent white booties with pink ribbon ties or a mobile from India festooned with little elephants. I would visit for a weekend, and the living-room couch would be concealed beneath an avalanche of stuffed animals and bright wooden blocks and rattles, and the freezer filled with sanitized baggies of mother's milk to be administered by baby-sitters and au pairs. These visits convinced me that the anxiety of aging can be tempered when you have children to give you an emphatic stake in the future. "This is my immortality," one woman told me, gazing at the sleeping infant in her lap.

I had never been sure I wanted children, though I was entirely sure that I wanted to choose whether I had them or not. In this choice, motherhood was not the issue. The issue was that unbreakable link between fertility and mortality. And in that sense, whether or not you had children was beside the point. The point was that one day you could no longer have them.

As it turned out in my own case, a few years after I made those eyelet curtains and the rag doll, I recognized that I would not be needing a layette or carefully compiled lists of preschools and baby-sitters.

If you had wanted a child, I told myself, you would have had one. Still, when it finally grew too late to have children, I grieved. Those of my friends who were parents felt sorry for me then, though in truth I did not grieve because I had no children. I grieved because I had no choice.

But that concept was too fearsome, so I concentrated instead on what I should do with the rag doll. I debated giving it away, but the gesture carried too much symbolic freight. Finally, I placed it in a closet in the New York apartment where I stored things that had not worked out in the upstate house where my husband still spent every possible moment and where I still never went.

The rag doll in the blue-and-white-checked muslin dress ended up on a shelf beside four panels of pale-gray vintage curtains from the 1940s adorned with mauve flowers. They were pretty curtains. I had had them for years and always liked them. Yet somehow, when I brought them to the country house, they had never looked quite right in any of the windows.

~ One month after I placed the rag doll in the closet, my husband took a suitcase from that same closet and packed in it all his clothes, including half a dozen Italian knit sweaters that had belonged to my grandfather.

That afternoon, he took the suitcase, his banjo, and his Gibson guitar to the vacant basement apartment of a man who had been his best friend since fourth grade.

Several weeks passed before either of us was able to admit that it would be better if he didn't come home again.

After that, I wondered, on occasion, if he wore my grandfather's sweaters on dates with other women.

22

~ Someone once told me that getting divorced is like cutting through a thick piece of rope composed of hundreds of tiny, twisted strands. Each of these strands binds you to the person whose coffee you prepared on countless mornings, with whom you waited in hospital corridors and airports at three in the morning.

You marry the person who makes you feel safe. You hope that each new love will be the last. Then you awaken one day and no longer feel safe, and you are on your own again.

~ After my marriage disintegrated, I began to notice the entropy at work in other people's domestic arrangements. There was the neglected wife of a prominent abstract expressionist who repaid this continuing lack of interest by bringing her lover to the opening of her husband's retrospective. There was the couple who railed mercilessly at each other in the presence of dinner guests in their insistently country kitchen, where a wall plaque read: "Recipe for a happy home: two cups of love, three dashes of trust, mixed with understanding."

When a marriage falls apart, acrimony is a useful tool. Where anger flourishes, pain has less room to exist. In that sense, these people were lucky. I would have been relieved had I been able to feel rage toward my husband or been capable of demonizing him. But I couldn't. The only anger I could muster was at myself.

It happened because it had to happen, someone said. I said this, too, because the lack of responsibility it implied made me feel better. But in those chill winter months following the breakup, I discovered what remorse is.

I would awaken when my windows were invaded by flat northern light, feeling dull and weary and sad. Scenes from early, promising days of the marriage remained fixed in my head as clear and specific as images and figures on a deck of cards. And I would shuffle through them, longtime player of a game of solitaire, trying to eke out a winning hand.

How do you get here from there? I wondered. Then my thoughts would proceed to that ever-expanding catalog of false moves and careless gestures I thought I could get away with but should never have allowed.

At night, in dreams, I flew in planes that were shot down. In my dreams, everything had a specific cost: Items sold for 51 cents or $11.99. These were the dreams of a person preoccupied with the unassailable fact that there is a price to be paid for everything.

∽ A marriage is not over simply because it ends. As with any amputation, it is followed by phantom pain. For months, I would walk past the storefront where we took the laundry or bought sourdough bread and think that while I gazed in this bakery window, he might be mowing the lawn or driving along the Taconic State Parkway or making love.

In shops I saw only things he would have admired: a well-worn violin case, a faded hooked rug. We had been together six years. In more respects than I had realized, I had come to see the world through his eyes. It would be a while before I saw through my own eyes again.

Here is another thing someone once told me: that love is the most difficult human transaction. But I don't think so. I think the most difficult transaction is letting go.

Letting go was mid-life's central gesture. You let go of people and you let go of expectations, and if you were lucky, you found a way to do it without letting go of hope.

23

~ Throughout the years I had lived in Los Angeles, I went home, to the East, twice each year, in December and in June. On these visits, I would study my grandmother's face. That she seemed to grow no older constituted a slight but significant trickery of time that profoundly pleased me.

"She hasn't changed," I recall telling my sister when my grandmother was eighty.

And I recall her answer: "You don't remember clearly."

~ Toward the end of an unusually bleak winter, when my grandmother was in her eighties, she and her younger sister went to Palm Beach, as they often had before. I have photographs of them on those earlier visits, poised on pink-and-white lounge chairs near the pool, paragons of beauty in mid-life, awash in the unapologetic self-absorption common to good-looking women, puffing on cigarettes, their tender white necks defended from the damning sun by pastel chiffon scarves. That was thirty years earlier. Now, my grandmother's sister was seventy-five, and one week after she arrived in Palm Beach, she went home to Philadelphia.

"She can't accept that the wonderful times are over," my grandmother said.

"But you have a wonderful time, don't you?" I asked.

"Are you kidding?" she replied. "At my age, nobody has a wonderful time. I have a nice time. I have a nice time watching other people have a wonderful time."

My grandmother's stay in Florida concluded several weeks later. When she returned home, I called again and asked what she was doing.

"You know what nothing is?" she said. "I'm doing nothing."

∾ Even then, my grandmother was beautiful, still the most glamorous person in a family in which looks had always mattered more than they should. She looked regal in restaurants or theaters or anyplace she could sit down. She wasn't regal standing up because she had become very small and had fallen several times and taken to walking with tiny, timorous steps. When I was learning to walk, she had guided me, but now it was she who was the unsteady one, and it was I who took her arm and did the guiding. To ease the discomfort generated by this turn of events, we tried joking about it.

"Don't you think you're old enough to learn to walk?" I would say.

"Not quite," she would answer, and we would pretend to laugh, and I would put my arm around her. My grandmother was smaller than I am, though possibly the most determined person I ever met. But her shoulders had come to feel bony and frail. She was old, and we were running out of time, for here, at the last, was something she could not overcome with determination.

I tried to memorize her features. I tried not to notice the age spots on her hands. I thought of nights I stayed with her when I was small, and the way she always tucked me into bed. I used to say, "See you in the morning."

And she would answer, "If all goes well."

Now I came to visit, stayed a few days, and then it was time to go.

"See you in June," I would say in December.

"See you in December," I would say in June.

But once I reached mid-life and she reached old age, neither of us said what had become too obvious to say: if all goes well.

∼ All went well for many years, and then it didn't anymore. Once, my grandmother had been exquisitely groomed, gracious, and well-informed. Now her clothes were spotted with little grease marks she could not see, and her bedside table was stacked with books she still made a point of buying but no longer read, and she nodded brightly while making a pretense of keeping up with conversations on topics she had ceased to follow.

When I was born, she was forty-two. In those days, her hair was marcel-waved and her pink lipstick perfectly applied. One of my early memories is of walking with her in Rittenhouse Square, where there would always be a passerby who was convinced she was Paulette Goddard.

I cannot pinpoint precisely when she began to fade, but along the way were the usual signs: the afternoon naps, the sudden, inexplicable moments of rage, the quiver of a mouth once firmly set.

Long before, she had told me that forty to sixty were the best years in a woman's life. I wanted to believe her, though I had begun to wonder what happens after sixty, especially now that she was in decline and I was embellishing a medical vocabulary, which already included useful terms like menopause and osteoporosis, with the names of other, less familiar age-related diseases like senile dementia.

And I could not watch my grandmother grow

old without perceiving her journey as a road map to my own future. For while I intended to be, at ninety, a spunky old lady who drove a red sports car and worked every day and flirted with sixty-year-old men, that was also the way I always envisioned old age for my grandmother. And when it did not turn out that way, this extinguished my hopeful faith that aging is only for others. Finally I knew that if I lived long enough, what had happened to her on the far side of mid-life would happen to me.

We begin helpless, we end helpless, and in between comes the struggle to prevail, the battle everyone ultimately loses but that the gifted and the beautiful appear to win, for a time.

When my grandmother seemed to be winning that struggle, she stored her silk stockings in monogrammed satin cases, soaked in rosewater-scented baths, and dominated a family of strong-minded people.

Like any formidable person who lives long enough, age gradually neutralized her, and the unabashed preferences and dislikes that had been so daunting were finally reduced to the harmless eccentricities of a very old woman.

My grandmother was in mid-life herself when President Franklin Roosevelt made the simple, astute observation that life is "iffy." But in the past, she had been far too bent on control to leave life in the hands of "ifs." And now it wasn't. Now she had left all traces of mid-life behind and was approaching the reckoning that has nothing to do with if and everything to do with when.

24

~ When my grandfather died, my grandparents had been married sixty-seven years. Their marriage had had its troubles, but they had been dedicated to one another. People said his death would kill her. She didn't die. Like him, she understood survival, and her particular response to overwhelming loss was courageous in its own way. She got her hair dyed platinum blond, bought a white angora sweater-and-skirt set, and went to Atlantic City in a chauffeured limousine with an eighty-nine-year-old real estate developer. "If I don't do what I want to do now," she asked me, "when am I going to do it?"

But then she fell again, and I took her to the hospital, and we sat on metal folding chairs while we waited for a doctor and she filled out the required forms. She wrote in her name, her address, declined to give her age, and when she reached the question about her occupation, she seemed perplexed. She thought a moment, then turned to me. "What was I?" she asked.

〜 We settled that day on *housewife*, though this word does not describe what she had become nearly so well as a story she once told me. Her father was a greengrocer, and when she was small he brought home a bag of apples. She bit into one and found a worm. Her father wouldn't let her throw the apple away. "If that apple's good enough for the worm, it's good enough for you," he told her.

"It was fruit," explained my grandmother. "That's what he sold. He wouldn't say anything bad about it. Listen, look, it's one of those things."

By the time she grew old, my grandmother had seen so much that she was long since inured to any eventuality. Divorce, death, disappointment—

all had equal standing and each was reduced, in her private computations, to being one of those things. And now, as another of those things, she was lying in a hospital bed, and we were both pretending nothing was wrong.

There was a tentative knock on her door, and then the door opened to reveal her caller, an elderly gentleman, slender and bald, dressed in a bright-red sweatshirt and red sweatpants. Confined to the same hospital, he was one of the few people still alive who could recall when five-course dinners at my grandmother's included sorbet refreshers and cut-crystal finger bowls on Irish-lace doilies.

He hesitated in the doorway, then beamed at her, and, executing a series of little soft-shoe steps, danced his way across the room, waving his cane, his slippered feet making a shuffling sound on the polished linoleum floor. When he reached her bedside, he stopped and looked down at her. The broad smile vanished and he burst into tears.

"Look at him," said my grandmother. "He doesn't know whether to laugh or cry."

She didn't seem to know which to do either, but I could see no point in mentioning it.

～ When my grandfather was alive, my grandmother and I always discussed what she should cook him for dinner. These conversations were lengthy, since we could both go on about whether salmon tasted better poached or steamed in foil and whether fresh dill-and-cucumber salad benefits more from red or vidalia onions. But with her husband dead, she lost interest in cooking, an unexpected development that effectively put an end to her one daily duty and, by extension, to ready topics for conversation.

From that point on, we talked about what had become most vivid to her, which is to say, we talked about the distant past.

That first afternoon in the hospital, she reminisced about working in Wanamaker's lingerie department when she was sixteen. It was a time when young people were both more responsible and more unworldly, and her watchful mother had met her for lunch each day at Gimbel's. "They had little tea sandwiches," my grandmother said. "I always thought it was so elegant."

After a while, she began to drift and soon grew fretful and agitated. "I made so many mistakes," she said.

And, of course, she had made many mistakes, including some that affected me, but if I had learned anything by then, it was that mistakes should be forgiven when it becomes too late for them to be rectified. And I did not want her to lie alone in a hospital bed, thinking of how she might have done things better.

"What mistakes?" I said. "Name one."

"I always thought it was so elegant," she finally said, "to eat at Gimbel's."

~ Visiting hours ended. A nurse said I should leave. Abandoning your family to the care of strangers is a knack most people acquire by mid-life, but a hard one to master, even with practice. I had not had much practice, and after I said good-bye, I got halfway down the hall, then turned back for one more moment.

My grandmother was staring at the wall. There were tears in her eyes. I would have asked what was wrong, but I knew what was wrong and knew that in any case she would never tell me. She belonged to a generation that asked for nothing, that derived honor from self-reliance.

I took her face in my hands. I looked in her eyes. She looked into mine. A long moment passed before she said, "Don't worry about me. I'm fine."

∽ She left the hospital a few weeks later, but then she fell again. That night, she tried getting up from her chair. A moment later, she tried again. She cried out, "What's going to become of me?" then instantly countered her own question.

"I won't think about it," she said, and you could see her gather herself together as she placed both hands decisively on the cane she now required. She forced herself up, commanding and intent, still capable of marshaling reserves of discipline. But after that day, her mind began to fade. I was convinced she willed the fading because she knew all too well what would become of her and did not want to witness it.

I did not want to witness it, either. Losing her would be a required loss, a predictable loss. I understood this, but I do not think that this understanding made it more bearable.

∾ Each time I visited my grandmother, I asked her advice about many things, because I always had and because I had been told that people live longer when they feel needed. In fact, I needed her. But she no longer wanted to be needed.

"I can't help you anymore," she said one day. "I'm too old. I'll be dead soon. It doesn't matter."

"It matters to me." I knew I shouldn't say this. I knew I should let her go. Yet I couldn't. Nor was I entirely convinced that it was what she wanted.

"I don't want to do it," she said one day.

"Are you talking about dying?" I asked.

"I think so," she said.

"You don't have to do it," I told her.

"I don't?" she said.

"Not now. You can stay with us awhile."

She took my hand and pressed it against her cheek. I loved this gesture. She never did it before she was bedridden, but after that, she did it often.

~ While my grandmother lay dying, I often sat beside her bed. To the railing of this bed, my sisters, my cousin, and I attached a small white teddy bear, a toy frog, a bouquet of pink silk flowers. I reached through the railing and held her hand. She spent her dying days watching television.

We watched soap operas and hockey games and any golf tournament in which the Australian golfer Greg Norman played. "That big blond hunk," my grandmother would say when he appeared on the screen. "I love him, I really do."

As the holidays neared, we watched cooking

shows. She lay in bed, her tiny head supported by two pillows with pale-blue cases, a woman who had loved to give lavish holiday parties but would never celebrate a holiday again, watching men in chef's toques and white aprons prepare turkey with three stuffings and plum pudding and a dish one cook described as "oysters Deauville with a festive garnish of salmon roe in breadcrumb-sprinkled filo."

She insisted on watching these cooking shows, but sometimes they saddened her, and I would not know what to say.

"It isn't important," I told her one day. "Things change—that's all."

"I know that," she said flatly. "I've caught on."

∿ In the final months of my grandmother's life, she became smaller and more frail. A series of minor strokes affected the part of the brain that accounts for unease and worry. After that, she often seemed happy—a bedridden, shrunken old lady whose nurse dressed her in pretty lace night-gowns and disposable diapers and who was not always certain who she was but whose perfect manners were always intact.

"How's my girlfriend?" the nurse asked one morning.

"Superb," said my grandmother.

She closed her eyes and seemed to sleep. Minutes passed. She opened her eyes again. "Why is this taking so long?" she asked.

~ **W**hat terrified me about my grandmother's condition was that this was as good as it gets. She was not sick. She was not in pain. She was simply old and had no teeth, and her legs looked like arms. Like everything else that had mattered to her, pride in her appearance had become a thing of the past.

By the time she took to her bed, she had lived so long that she had to be spoon-fed, and her daughter and granddaughters were stocking her refrigerator with baby food. We would go to the

Spruce Market, where she had once ordered legs of lamb and prime ribs of beef, and buy her nourishing drinks sold at a display stand with a sign that read: Insure Your Baby's Future.

And by the end, I came to love my grandmother in the way a mother loves a newborn child. I expected nothing from her but was delighted that I could make her smile, that she recognized me and was aware that we had a common history.

Yet even after she entered this state, she had a quality shared by the dying that makes you think they know things you don't. And I would sit by her bed, whose chrome railing made it resemble a crib, and wonder if she would suddenly tell me things that would make it easier to live my life. But as it turned out, my grandmother had questions, not answers.

"There's something I don't understand," she said.

I asked what it was, but she didn't know.

"I just don't understand," she said again. And so it fell to me to explain things to her. The only explanation I could summon was pretty simple.

"You don't have to understand everything," I told her. "Nobody does."

In some obscure way, that seemed to satisfy her.

"There's an idea," she said.

She fell asleep. I sat beside her bed and watched her. Each time she exhaled, her cheeks filled with air, and for that moment her face became full and she looked like the woman I remembered from days when I wore smocked dresses and white ankle socks and she was mistaken for Paulette Goddard by strangers in Rittenhouse Square. Then she inhaled and her cheeks sank in and she looked once more like the dying old lady she had become.

~ A month before my grandmother died, the younger of my two sisters visited her from California. We were about to leave for dinner when it became clear that our grandmother didn't want us to go. And so we ordered in from a nearby restaurant. We pretended that she could eat more than

baby food and ordered three crab-salad sandwiches, three strawberry milkshakes, and three
slices of angel cake with orange icing. "It'll be the
end of us," said my grandmother, "but what a way
to go."

We stayed with her until midnight. "It doesn't
matter," she whispered as we were leaving, "that
it's a little late."

"Late at night," I asked, "or in life?"

"In life," she said.

"But we're still here," my sister told her.
"We'll have good times."

"Oh, sure," she whispered, "lots of good
times."

$\sim$ I do not know when I allowed myself to accept that my grandmother wanted to die. I only
know that I finally recognized that she was living
only because she was afraid to relinquish her hold
and that she had arrived at the point where that
final letting go ceases to be the last defeat and
becomes its own kind of victory.

165

She wanted to die, and I tried to ease her through it. I told her that everyone loved her, that her family was fine, that she had completed her job and could rest. Each time I tried to ease her through it, I felt lonely and afraid, because I was learning what dying is, and because the possibility existed that my efforts might succeed.

To witness a death is to endure an intimacy that binds you to the most fundamental of collective experiences. In half-lit rooms throughout the world, at every moment of the day and night, sorrowing people seek to retain composure, while keeping vigil over someone who soon will disappear forever.

My thoughts kept returning to a woman I knew whose dying mother had gone blind. "You don't have to hold on anymore," she told her. "Go free, to where you can see a hundred miles in every direction."

Then the woman died, and her fifty-five-year-old daughter left the hospital alone, carrying with her a bag that held her mother's nightclothes and slippers. Then she drove home, and once inside, phoned her mother's empty apartment so she could hear her voice on the answering machine.

～ On our last day together, my grandmother did not speak, but her blue eyes remained fixed on a turquoise bracelet I was wearing.

As I left for the final time, I took this bracelet from my wrist and fastened it to the guardrail of her bed so that it would be in her line of vision.

She grasped my hand. There had been so many fervent handclasps before. We had said good-bye so many times.

We had spent years rehearsing for this moment and still were not ready for it when it came.

～ Then she was dead, and men from the funeral home took away her body. Once they were gone, the hospital bed with the pale-blue sheets was empty. But there remained, on a pillow, a small oval-shaped indent where her head had been. My mother straightened the sheets. She picked up the pillow. When she set the pillow down again, the oval-shaped indent was gone.

~ After my grandmother died, I discovered in her china closet a white dish, edged in gold, rectangular in shape, with three porcelain fish on its lid. It is, I have been told, the dish in which she served sardines, and I found it an oddly appealing relic from a vanished era when upward mobility was the way of things and people took pride in knowing what was proper.

My grandmother was a student of such mannerly ways, though where she learned them I do not know. Her people were Romanian horse thieves. But they arrived in the new land and tidied up their ways, and by the time I was born, my grandmother was setting her table with Irish linen and English china.

Now that she was gone, those possessions were divided. My mother took the linens. I took the china. I look at that china and know that someday I will be the one who leaves it behind. Other people will have it then. And it will be for them what it is for me: a keepsake of someone who has died.

So it has been and will always be.

Things last longer than people.

25

~ Thirty years after my high school graduation, the annual alumni list arrived in the mail. This list offered the usual assortment of current facts and figures about women dimly remembered for winning the biology prize or flunking Latin or smoking Newports in the bathroom. There were new addresses on better suburban streets, job promotions, and, in the wake of what some breezily dismissed as "divorce number two," the resumption of maiden names.

In my high school class, there were twenty-six women. Thirty years after graduation, a word not previously attached to any of their names appeared beside one of them. That word startled me, though

I understood it had been destined to turn up sooner or later. The word was *deceased*.

The woman who died had been one of the C students, pleasant if unremarkable, neither particularly pretty nor bright. Death, as it sometimes does, had imbued her with a mystique that eluded her in life, and once I knew she was dead, I found myself thinking of her, wondering what had happened and wondering if you have time to come to terms with things when you are given only thirty years after high school graduation to do it.

∼ Yet by then, I had begun to come to terms with things myself. This settlement occurred for a number of reasons, among them that protracted exposure to the business of dying tends to rouse the living to make the best of things. Beyond that, it happened because entering mid-life is a process, one guided, like any process, by implacable dictates and rhythms.

When mid-life begins, it is like being forsaken

at some perilous midpoint between age and youth, between the future and the past. It is like standing on a fault line, the familiar earth shifting beneath your feet as you attempt to seek balance on two wavering land plates that can only move farther apart. And you remain there, knowing that you must negotiate the seemingly impassable distance from one of these land plates to the other.

When this process began, I would find myself in the ballet classes I took several days a week, a despondent woman in a leotard, practice skirt, and ragged pink dancing slippers, in no way prepared to be the oldest person in the room. In this precarious state, I could only envy all those young girls with their lives before them.

After a time, my perceptions changed. Matters that had troubled me no longer did. This improved condition was not preceded by any great event, unless you regard the ordinary passage of time as a great event. It was simply that I had acclimatized to being older, in the process discovering that entering mid-life is like sustaining a prolonged shock that finally subsides.

During this time, I was asked to write about Mikhail Baryshnikov, that most exquisite of dancers, who had, in the course of his own mid-life, grown too old to maintain his meticulous standards in classic ballet.

"Will you dance Albrecht in *Giselle* one more time?" I heard a fan ask him.

"For you, it's one more time," he told her. "For me, it's months of preparation."

In his youth, Baryshnikov had rarely enjoyed dancing. Now he was in his forties and had just formed a modern dance troupe and was doing anything he could to go on dancing, because the lack of time in which to do it had made it more meaningful. "It gets sweeter," I recall him saying.

And by then, I had begun to perceive that everything gets sweeter because everything ends. That is the ultimate barter. "This thou believest," Shakespeare wrote, "which makes thy love more strong—to love that well which thou must leave 'ere long."

And so I became reconciled to the way of things. Because you do reconcile. You accept that youth fades away, just as you eventually accept that experience is finite and that you can't have everything.

Among those things I had always wanted was to bridge the distance long ago established between my father and myself. And I had nurtured the hope that someday we would set off together on the revelatory fishing trip or walk in Fairmount Park during which confidences would be exchanged and understandings reached.

But when I began coming to terms with things, I realized that this might never come to pass. Yet if that was to be another loss, it would at least be one that freed me, for better and worse, to romanticize the charming, handsome father who once took me to the zoo, and to the child that I was then, seemed so very big and strong.

My father is in his late seventies now. Each time I see him, I'm surprised that he's not taller.

~ There were fissures in relation to my mother too, though I knew her more completely. I still recall how much I wanted her with me during a troubled time when I was in my thirties. I called her in New York, and a day later she flew out to Los Angeles and we took a room overlooking the Pacific in the old Miramar Hotel. The next morning, I woke before she did and lay in bed, listening to her breathe as she slept in a narrow bed on the other side of the night table. My mother had come three thousand miles. Now she was five feet from me. Yet the wish to commune with parents can be so sharp, so profound, that however close we venture, it still may seem that it is not near enough.

As my own parents grew older, both developed a desire to travel, and they would set off with their respective spouses to the Greek Isles, or St. Petersburg, or Pisa, maintaining rigorous schedules that made them inaccessible.

When they were gone, I was always surprised by how much I missed them. I would long to talk to them. And not being able to do so gave me a taste of what it will be like later.

26

~ By the time the movies my husband and I had seen together began coming out on video, he and I were making an effort to be friends. We became as friendly as it is possible to be with a person who has judged you and found you wanting.

Yet along the way, there was what is generally known as a healing process, though once again, the primary element in this process was time. In time, I grew accustomed to the fact that he and his wife spent weekends and summers in the house upstate, erstwhile dream house of our erstwhile marriage, for which I supplied half the down payment.

But every so often, we would have a conversation that would remind me of why we had married and why we had reason to hope our marriage

would last. After one of these dialogues, I walked
him to the subway, and just before he boarded his
train, we held each other for an instant. There was
no longing and no passion. There was simply an
enveloping sadness, and the only way I could deal
with it was to be flip.

"What a mess I am," I said. "I got lipstick on
your nice jacket."

"You gave me the jacket," he answered.

"I know," I said.

∾ I have tried, since then, to note the mistakes
I made in that marriage, an exercise undertaken
partially in a spirit of self-recrimination but also in
the more useful belief that to recognize one's er-
rors is to not repeat them. My former husband did
this, too. And so we constituted for one another a
sort of practice run, in which both partners iden-
tify what they must never do again.

In truth, a long time passed before I could
bear doing any of it again, the starting fresh, en-
listing hope, committing to memory the names of

yet another partner's birthplace and favorite aunt and childhood pets. But sooner or later we go on, because it is the way of things. And because we do, in fact, learn from our mistakes, the next time is often better.

Eventually, I began to see another man, who had a past to learn from, too, and now we live in a house full of relics from those former incarnations: my grandmother's gold and white sardine dish, his crystal paperweights and framed original costume sketch from Coppelia.

In my old country house, there may still be a coffee mug bought in Memphis after my husband and I drove there on a dusty, scorching August day. Late that night, we bought a bag of Krispy Kreme donuts and then stood outside the Graceland gate, indulging in what we called the Elvis Presley Memorial Binge. That was a good night, and the next morning we bought the mug at Souvenirs of Elvis on Elvis Presley Boulevard. Now his wife may drink her coffee from it, just as I drink from mugs purchased on someone else's good nights and days at the London Zoo and Charleston's Spoleto Festival and other places I have never been.

In any case, moving in with this man taught me that to begin anew in mid-life is to share the franchise to your own existence: to sleep in a house you did not choose, to make slipcovers for a couch you did not buy, to select sweater vests and bathrobes for children you did not have, and, in general, to recognize that adult people arrive with established bonds that run long and deep.

Yet one aspect of a love affair remains immaculate and fresh, and it is, perhaps, the most vital of all: the wish that here, finally, is the love that will not break down into those two distinct and familiar phases, at first and at last.

27

⁓ These days, I look forward to the future, though I still mourn, at times, for the past. Among the enduring human sorrows is the longing for a time gone by. To some extent, we are all Edward Arlington Robinson's Miniver Cheevy, who was "born too late" and "mourned the days when swords were bright and knights were dancing."

And we are all in concord with Yeats, who pined for the stately order of the century previous. "For how but in custom and in ceremony," he wrote, "are innocence and beauty born?"

That sense is inescapable. It is the stuff of wishing, of wanting, a yearning present even in our sleep. In this regard, I recall a long ago day when my great-grandfather was found searching through closets in my grandmother's apartment. By then, his mind had faded, and she asked what he was seeking.

"A *nechtiker tog,*" he answered. He used these Yiddish words to mean "the lost day." For years after I heard this story, I pictured my great-grandfather searching for that lost day in closets stuffed with fleece-lined winter coats and discarded golf clubs and Monopoly boards. Still, I see him as no more pitiable than anyone else. The lost day, ever enchanted, ever elusive, is what everyone seeks and no one finds.

And so we mourn the good old days and forget that those days are a mirage. Good old days are never as good when they are new. The past grows brighter as time proceeds, because we have learned that we can live with what it was leading us to.

～ *Nothing gold can stay.* This no longer strikes me as sad. I suppose that if you live long enough, what once seemed sad comes to seem natural. And I suppose that, having lived long enough to persist through the variant phases of life and benefit from all of them, your conception of "gold" is bound to change. For to accept that each successive stage of living has its value and its price is to accept that nothing gold *should* stay.

Which is why there is no sadness in thinking that once I was young and now I am not. And it is why there need be no sadness in thinking that those who currently are young will cease to be young, too.

Life being what it is, they will have weathered much by then, and having done so, they will, perhaps, obtain solace from knowing what I have come to know, which is that life can be weathered.

And while I always assumed that when I reached mid-life, I would not want to think about my own mortality, I find I want to think about it now. I want to because I'm one more person who elevated procrastination and sloth into an art through sheer dint of practice. Yet these days, I have no patience with sloth, and I don't procrastinate much, and I try not to waste time. My life has improved accordingly. I'm not surprised. I've always been one of those people who does better on a deadline.

And though I still make mistakes, I am less inclined to delude myself about their cost. I no longer expect things to make sense. I know there is no safety. But that does not mean there is no magic. It does not mean there is no hope.

It simply means that each of us has reason to be wishful and frightened, aspiring and flawed.

And it means that to the degree that we are lost, it is on the same ocean, in the same night.

Acknowledgments

A book draws on the energies of many people. *Mid-life* grew from a lunch with a particularly gifted editor, Adam Moss, and would not exist without his initial enthusiasm and encouragement. Nor would it exist without the unwavering faith of my agent, Richard Pine, and the early, strong support of Joni Evans and Liz Perle McKenna. In a more general sense, I am indebted to the tremendous intelligence and loyalty of the editors of *Esquire*, and particularly of David Hirshey.

Mid-life also benefited from the steadfast assistance of Lori Andiman, the ministrations of Phoebe Payaqui, the insight of Thomas Kranjac, the tireless research of Andrew Chaikivsky, the copy editing of John Kenney, and the expert burnishing of Linda Nardi. And I was blessed with an editor of inordinate intelligence, focus, and generosity, Nancy Miller.

Three friends read the final manuscript and improved it with incisive comments: Peggy Kaye, Ann Hornaday, and David Gates. Above all, I am indebted to Clive Barnes, for his editorial wisdom and for living through the process with me.